Table of Contents (cont.)

Plays

Introduction

Welcome to *Quick & Easy Costumes and Plays*. This book contains everything you need to help your class successfully put on a play. There are 11 plays and 22 patterns for all the costumes needed. Each play lists the necessary props and gives clear stage directions.

Why Use Plays?

Using plays in your curriculum enriches your students' learning by providing these benefits:

- enhancing literacy through repeated readings of text

- promoting visualization by seeing the text come to life

- strengthening students' understanding of plot and story development

- giving realistic experience performing before an audience

- providing experience being members of an audience

- showing the behind-the-scenes efforts and details that go into a theatrical production

- developing an appreciation for theater

- improving class cohesiveness and creating a teamwork atmosphere

Role-Playing

Role-playing for children is a natural, enjoyable expression of feelings, experiences, and fantasies. Children love to role-play. They are born actors who should be encouraged to act out the characters and plots to stories, real or make-believe. The synthesis of skills involved in such activities powers the children's understanding of themselves and others. Sympathy, compassion, humor, and affection are among the enduring qualities children learn to develop and expand through role-playing. Add to these qualities the child's growing fluency of expression—verbal and physical—that springs naturally from adopting the persona of different characters. The sum can only be a great and growing self-confidence genuinely earned by the child's increased mastery of language, self, and situation.

Costuming

Costumed children who perform before their families and friends are inevitably provided with fun-filled, memorable experiences. The preparation, the anticipation, the actual performances—all provide immediate and recalled senses of accomplishment and joy.

This book provides easy-to-follow and cost-efficient patterns and directions to help teachers quickly create costumes for their plays. Rather than masks, most of these costumes use headpieces which enable children to speak, sing, and see without restriction. Also, each child is identifiable to the guests (including proud parents) in the audience.

Occasionally the patterns in this book will need to be enlarged. Sometimes this can be done on a photocopier. You can also use an overhead projector. Make a transparency of the costume pattern, then project it onto a blank wall. Move the projector until you get the desired size. Next, tack up a large piece of white tagboard, construction paper, or butcher paper, and trace the enlarged costume piece(s) onto it.

Contributing Authors
Joyce Combes, Nathaniel Combes, and Priya Patel

Editor
Walter Kelly, M.A.

Editorial Project Manager
Ina Massler Levin, M.A.

Editor in Chief
Sharon Coan, M.S. Ed.

Illustrator
Bruce Hedges

Cover Artist
Jeff Sutherland

Art Coordinator
Denice Adorno

Creative Director
Elayne Roberts

Imaging
Stephanie A. Salcido

Product Manager
Phil Garcia

Publishers
Rachelle Cracchiolo, M.S. Ed.
Mary Dupuy Smith, M.S. Ed.

Author

Debra J. Housel, M.S. Ed.

Teacher Created Materials, Inc.
6421 Industry Way
Westminster, CA 92683
www.teachercreated.com

ISBN-1-57690-356-7

©*2000 Teacher Created Materials, Inc.*
Reprinted, 2000
Made in U.S.A.

Table of Contents

Introduction *(cont.)*

Selecting a Play

When choosing a play for your class, be sure to consider the curricular impact as well as the students' interests and reading abilities. In order to promote ownership and pride, it is a good idea, if feasible, to get student input when selecting a play.

The plays with the simplest dialogue and the fewest lines per actor are the easiest for young children to perform. Some of the best choices for early childhood through grade one are *A Celebration of Nursery Rhymes*, *Aesop's Fables*, and *Bee-ing a Bee*.

Adapt the plays in any way that benefits your class. For example, if a kindergarten class wants to do *The Three Billy Goats Gruff*, the teacher or an older student can read the narrator's part. Prepare children to anticipate the dialogue and action by reading *The Three Billy Goats Gruff* and doing extension activities. If there are too many lines for a child to memorize, split the part—for example, have three narrators instead of one. Also, not all parts must be memorized; it's okay to have children read from the script in informal productions.

For plays that do not have enough parts for the entire class, you may want to have two or three separate casts. Each cast then performs for the others. Or you can select several plays and have each group perform for the rest of the class.

For the most part, the roles in each play can be portrayed by either boys or girls unless, of course, the role is obviously gender-specific as in the case of a king or queen.

Scene Changes

Keep scene changes simple. In ancient Japan, scene and prop changes were effected by stagehands dressed in black—like shadows, not calling attention to themselves. Your class may choose to use this technique for your important stage crew. If the scene change is simple, such as adding a chair or removing an item or two, the stagehand simply slips onto the stage between scenes and adds or removes the necessary props.

If the scene change is quite large, however, such as the outdoor forest scene in Scene I and the indoor scene in Scene II of *Goldilocks and the Three Bears*, a decision will have to be made between closing the curtains to make the change or keeping it very simple by using the walk-on-walk-off method of scene change.

Introduction *(cont.)*

Scene Changes *(cont.)*

New background scenes will be done on large, but manageable, pieces of sturdy butcher paper. Roll the scene like a horizontal scroll attached to two poles. Two stagehands (one at each pole) will carry the scene to the stage. Mark the stage floor where they will stand and unroll to present the new scene. It does not matter if parts of another scene are partially visible, as we want to just create the illusion of the scene change. It is important that the poles be the same length and that the scene be attached to the poles at the same mark so that the scene is straight when the poles are set down. Setting the poles down will make it easier for the stagehands to keep the scene straight and steady. An additional center pole may be added to give more support to your background.

Materials

Materials used for the costumes are used daily in most classrooms. Make sure you have the following available:

- construction paper, wide variety of colors
- tagboard
- butcher paper
- brass paper fasteners, ³/₄ inch (2 cm) size
- rubber bands, various sizes
- all-purpose white glue
- stapler
- scissors
- thick markers and classroom paint
- large safety pins
- yarn and twine used for fastening
- masking tape
- safety pins
- black pipe cleaners or chenille sticks
- optional embellishments—feathers, rhinestones, beads, sequins, and other decorative costume elements

Rehearsing

First, have the students read through the script at least three times to familiarize them with the story. Next, assign parts. With older children, you may want to have auditions. Proceed with blocking—that is, showing children when and how to enter and exit—while they are still reading from their scripts.

Allow at least 20 minutes a day for at least a month to prepare for a play. For younger children or a more challenging play, give at least six weeks. If giving up class time is not feasible, you may be able to have rehearsals before or after school.

Introduction *(cont.)*

Rehearsing *(cont.)*

If at all possible, do the rehearsing when you have adult assistance, whether it be a student teacher, a parent volunteer, or a teacher's aide. Have the helper take a portion of the class and do an activity with them while you coach the actors. Or, if all the children are to perform, split them according to the act(s) they are in. Then you and your helper can each take a group and go over a specific act or scene with them.

Have at least two dress rehearsals.

Non-Acting Roles

Students can contribute their talents to a play in the following ways:

- Director
- Props Manager
- Lighting Manager
- Costume Manager
- Program Manager

- Sound Effects Manager
- Scenery Designer
- Publicity Manager
- Ushers
- Stage Hands

Putting On the Play

Putting on a play for another class, the whole school, or even the entire community requires planning and organization. Here are the steps to follow to have a successful production:

1. At least two months prior to the performance, choose the play and conduct three or more read-through sessions.
2. Select a cast.
3. Decide which, if any, of the parts must be memorized. Send home copies of the play with the child's part highlighted, and enlist the parents' help in memorization.
4. Prepare the costumes.
5. Begin the rehearsals. As soon as possible, move the rehearsals to the stage or designated area where the play will actually be presented.
6. Create the scenery and collect the necessary props. Children generally enjoy making the backdrops and other pieces of scenery whenever possible. Sometimes other faculty members and parents can provide props.
7. Have the children design posters and flyers advertising the play. Attach the flyers to school newsletters and mount the posters on school walls.
8. Design and print a program. The program usually lists the acts and the names of the cast, behind-the-scenes workers, and people who deserve thanks (and for what).
9. If desired, incorporate lighting and sound effects.
10. Conduct a dress rehearsal WITHOUT stopping for errors. Discuss mistakes and changes; then do another dress rehearsal.
11. Above all, make this a fun-filled, memorable experience for the children. For many people, school plays remain their favorite school memories. This is far more important than a "flawless" production.

Basic Patterns

The use of basic patterns which can be adapted to many different plays is the most flexible way to costume your class with a limited budget and limited preparation time. Moreover, it has been found that upper grade children will not hesitate to use their creativity to design their very own special characteristics. As the teacher, you will benefit by using these basic patterns to begin with and later embellishing and building upon the base as desired. Be creative!

Headpiece

Create the basic headpiece by following the directions and diagram below.

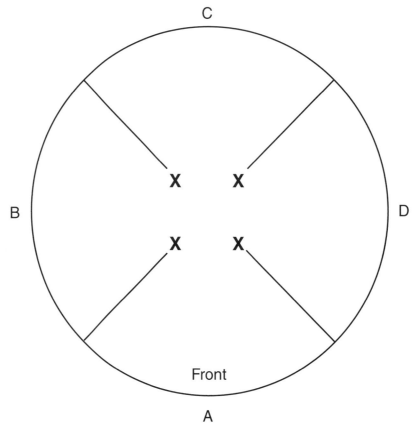

1. Trace and cut a circle on construction paper.
2. Cut on each of the four lines leading to the center. Stop at each X. Do not cut completely to the center.
3. Fold, overlap, and staple to form a cap to fit the child's head. Make sure it sits well.

   - Looking at the circle with flap A facing you, slightly overlap the left side of flap A over the right side of flap B and staple the two together.
   - In the same manner, overlap the right side of flap A over the left side of flap D and then staple the two together.
   - Now overlap the unattached sides of flaps B and D over flap C and staple both sides together.

This should form a cap to fit the child's head. Section A becomes the front of the cap. Use the pattern on page 9 to serve as one quarter of a full-size circle to trace four times onto construction paper (or tagboard if you want a sturdier base).

Basic Patterns *(cont.)*

Headpiece *(cont.)*

Directions: Trace this quarter circle four times on a large piece of construction paper and follow directions on page 8 to compete the basic headpiece.

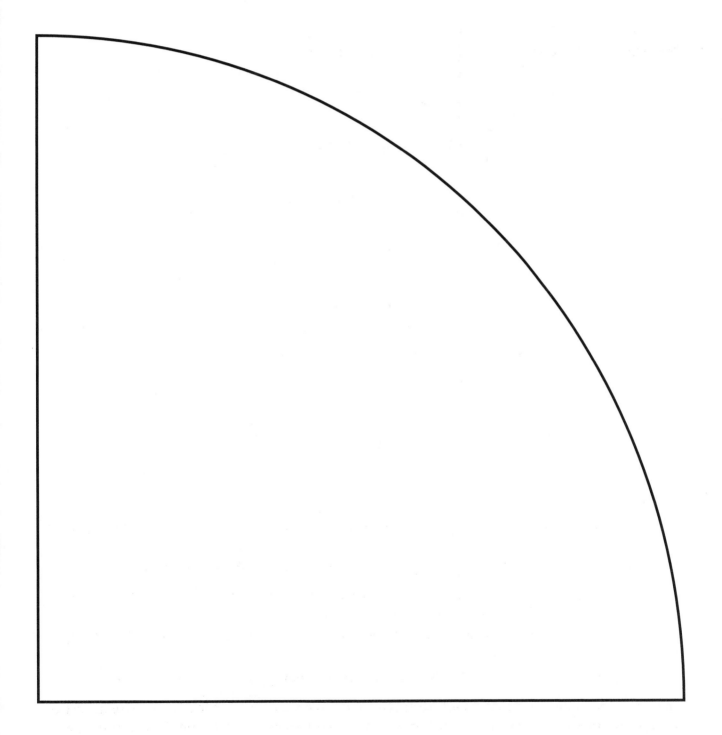

Basic Patterns *(cont.)*

Body Vest

Create the basic body vest by following the directions and diagrams below.

1. Cut pattern A on folded tagboard and open up.

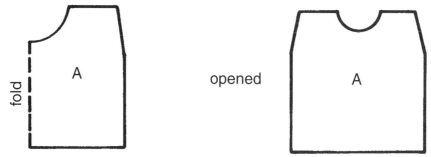

2. Cut pattern B on folded tagboard and open up. Glue pattern A to the top of pattern B, overlapping the tab spaces.

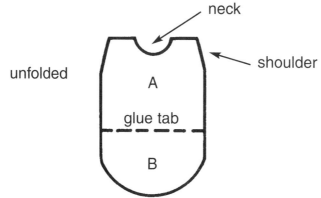

3. Use the assembled tagboard pattern to cut body vests of desired colors from construction paper or butcher paper. Cut a front and back for each character.

4. Place the shoulders of the pattern on the fold of a doubled piece of butcher paper or construction paper.

5. Cut out and then split the back of the vest, punch holes at reinforced edges at the top, and use ties to fit the completed vest to the actor.

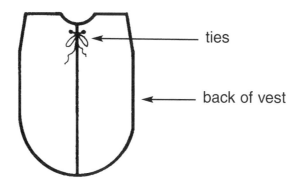

See pages 11 and 12 for quarter panels of patterns A and B to trace onto tagboard. These may need to be enlarged slightly, depending on the sizes of your students. Use a copy machine or overhead projector to enlarge.

Basic Patterns *(cont.)*

Body Vest *(cont.)*

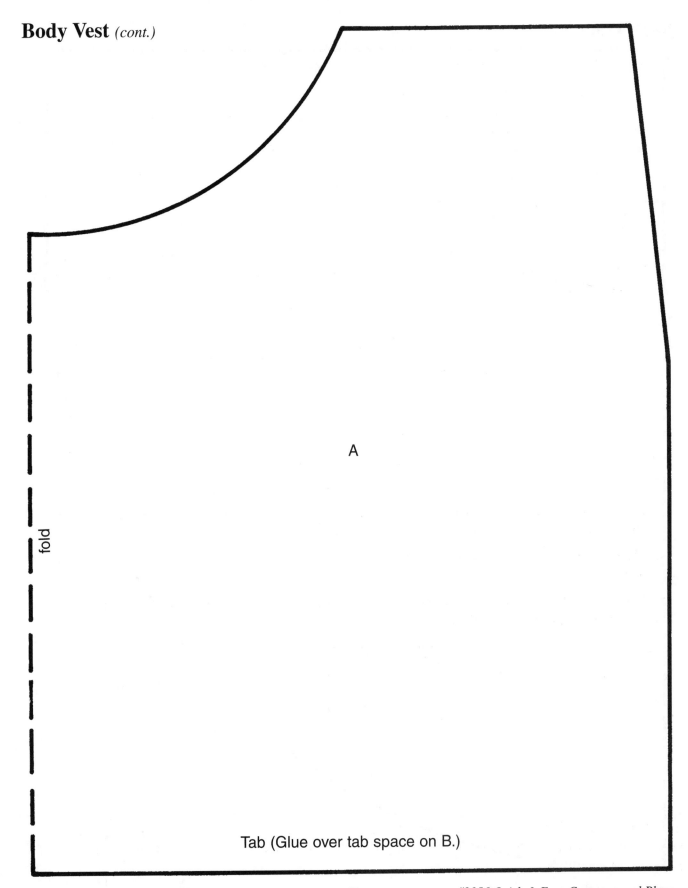

fold

A

Tab (Glue over tab space on B.)

Basic Patterns *(cont.)*

Body Vest *(cont.)*

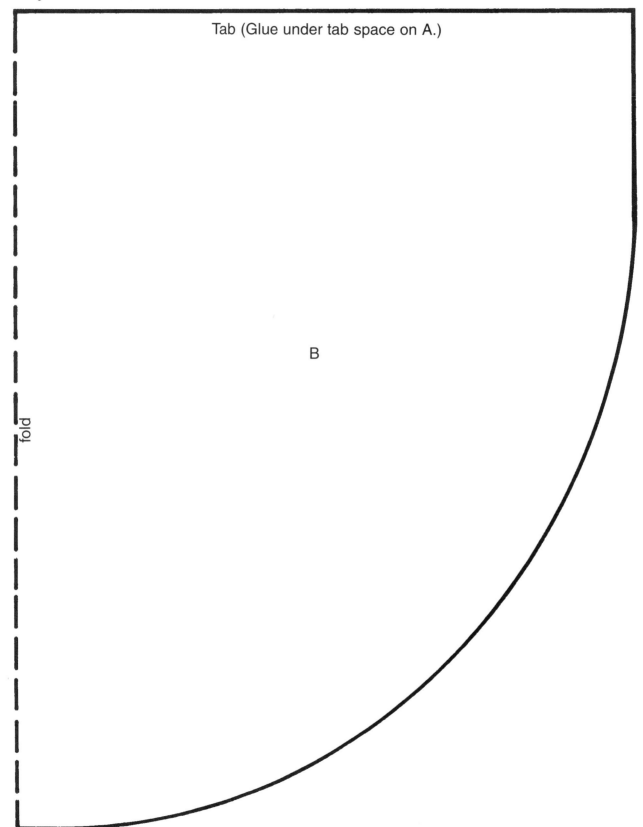

Tab (Glue under tab space on A.)

fold

B

Basic Patterns *(cont.)*

Wings

Create the basic wings by following the directions and diagrams below.

1. Glue the top (A) and bottom (B) of the wing patterns together onto tagboard, cut out, and use this as the pattern to trace onto construction paper for the actual wings.

2. The rounded side of the wing faces front. Make one for the left arm and one for the right.

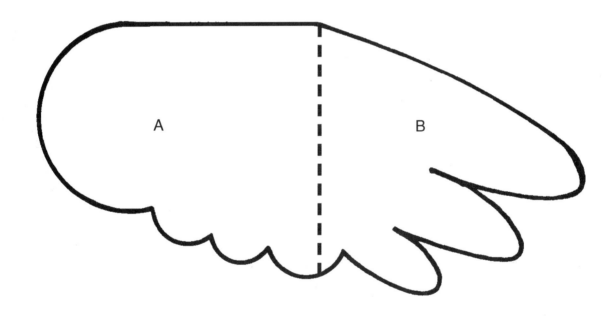

3. With masking tape or duct tape, reinforce the top where the hole is to be punched. Punch the hole. Secure the wings with safety pins onto the actor's clothing. They seem to look best when pinned to the seam between sleeve and shoulder.

Top and bottom half-wing parts for placing onto tagboard appear on pages 14 and 15. They may need to be enlarged slightly, depending on the sizes of your students.

See page 16 for patterns and directions for creating the feathers to complete the wings.

Basic Patterns *(cont.)*

Wings *(cont.)*

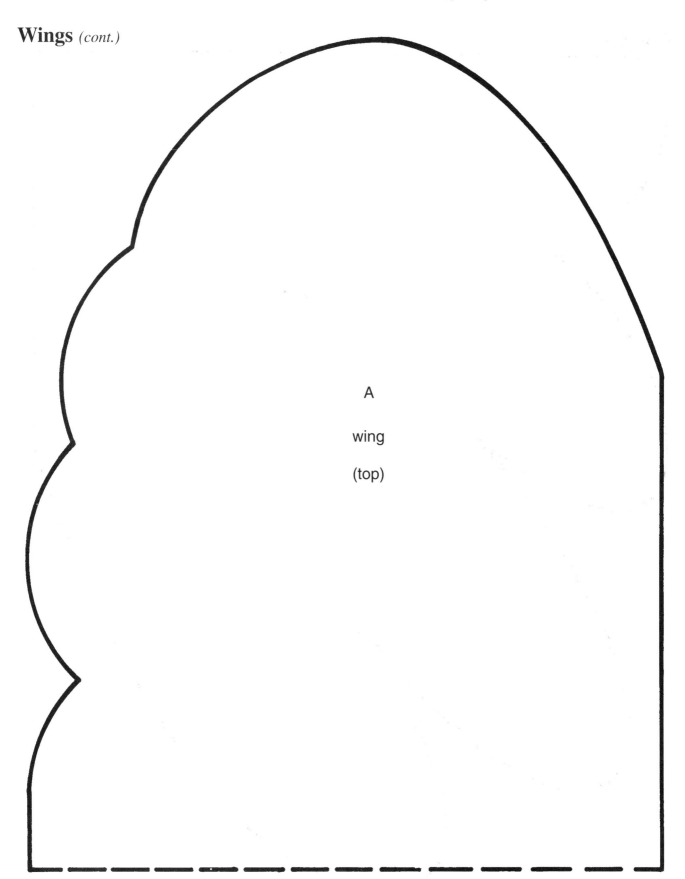

A

wing

(top)

Basic Patterns *(cont.)*

Wings *(cont.)*

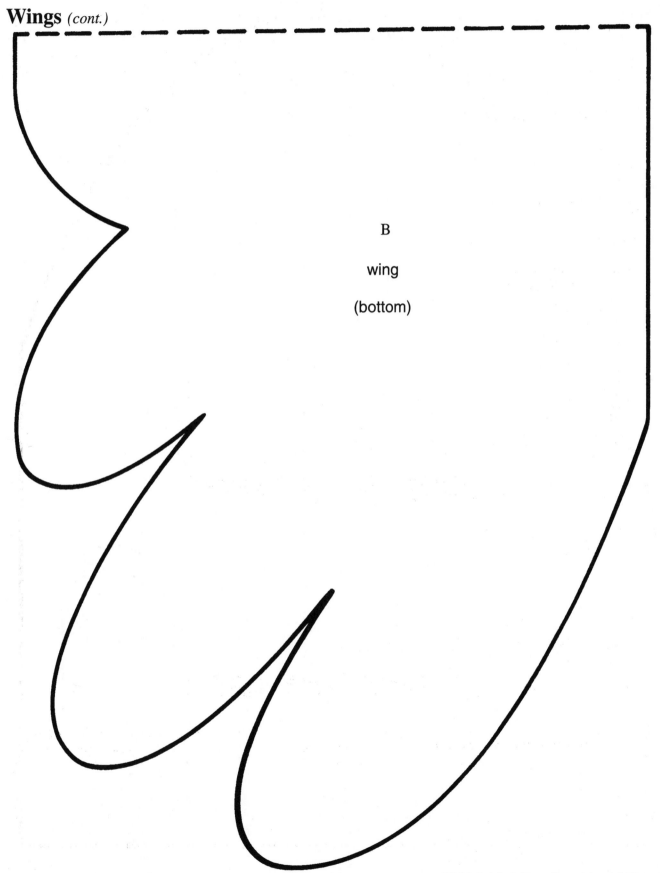

B

wing

(bottom)

Basic Patterns *(cont.)*

Wings *(cont.)*

To create wing feathers, follow the directions and diagrams below.

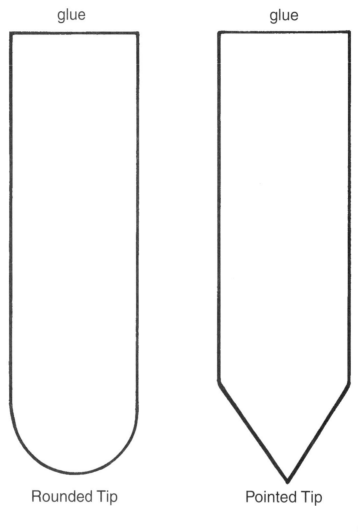

glue   glue

Rounded Tip   Pointed Tip

1. Cut 40 to 45 rounded or pointed tipped feathers for each wing. Make one left and one right for each pair.

2. Curl the tips of each feather by rolling the tips onto a pen or pencil.

3. Glue only the straight end onto the wing. The rounded or pointed tip should be left unglued to curl.

4. Construction paper and butcher paper curl nicely, but you may wish to experiment with other materials to get the look you want. Other materials to simulate feathers might include gold or silver foil, ribbons, tissue paper, etc. (When stage lighting is used, gold and silver foil along with glitter and threading are very striking.)

Hens

(Little Red Hen)

1. The basic headpiece is made of light brown or tan construction paper.

2. Wings are made to match. (See basic patterns for wings.)

3. Beak, wattle, and crown patterns are on pages 18 and 19.

Assembly

1. Construct the headpiece. Except for the face area, cover the headpiece with real brown and orange feathers.

2. Cut a pair of wings to match. Cover the wings with feathers to match the headpiece.

3. Attach the beak, wattle, crown, and eyes.

4. Have the child wear a brown T-shirt or sweatshirt.

Hens *(cont.)*

(Little Red Hen)

Crown

1. Cut the crown out of bright red construction paper.

2. The crown is constructed out of three pieces to more easily fit into the curve at the top of the headpiece.

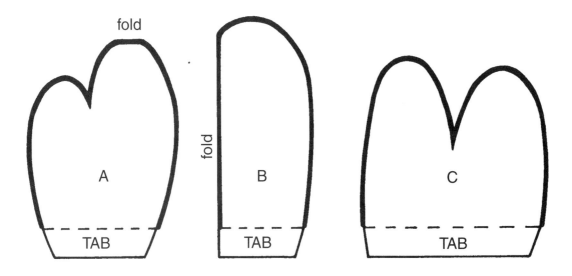

3. Cut a slit about six inches (15 cm) long, front to back, at the top on the headpiece.

4. Insert A in the front. Add B with the folded side in front, and then insert it between the cut folds of A at an angle. Bend the bottoms of A and B under the headpiece and tape them securely to hold. Fit in C and tape it in place.

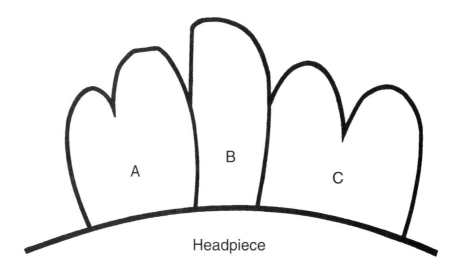

Hens *(cont.)*

(Little Red Hen)

Beak and Wattle

1. Cut the beak on a fold of orange construction paper.

2. Glue the beak to the headpiece.

3. Make a vertical crease on the top piece of the beak.

4. Twist a strip of red tissue paper to form a wattle about five inches (12.5 cm) long. Glue it over the top of the beak and let it hang at the side.

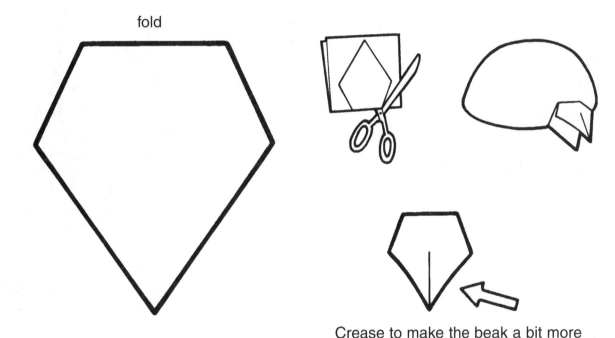

fold

Crease to make the beak a bit more three-dimensional.

Chicks

For each chick, you will need the following items:

1. one yellow headpiece

2. a pair of yellow wings

3. an orange beak (See Little Red Hen pattern.)

4. expressive eyes (page 20)

5. a yellow body vest (See Basic Patterns.)

6. yellow T-shirt or sweatshirt to wear underneath the body vest

Ducks

For each duck or duckling, you will need the following items:

1. one basic headpiece (The colors most often used are white, yellow, brown, and black. A mallard duck could be constructed from tan construction paper with the greens, blacks, and whites painted on.)

2. a pair of wings

3. an orange bill (See pattern on page 22.)

4. expressive eyes, with or without lashes (Cut a pair of eyes out of construction paper, and paint pupils black or cut them from black construction paper.)

Ducks *(cont.)*

Assembly

1. Construct the headpiece.

2. Cut an orange bill (two pieces—top and bottom).

3. Assemble the bill by putting the top piece, which is slightly wider than the bottom one, over the bottom piece. Align the left sides and staple. Then align the right sides and staple. This should create a slight pucker or bulge at the top.

4. Insert the edge of a headpiece between the top and bottom layers of the bill and the pointed or back end.

5. Create or use patterns for expressive eyes (page 20).

6. Use the body vests of matching color.

7. Have the children wear T-shirts or sweatshirts the color of their ducks or ducklings (white shirts for white ducks, etc.) under the body vests.

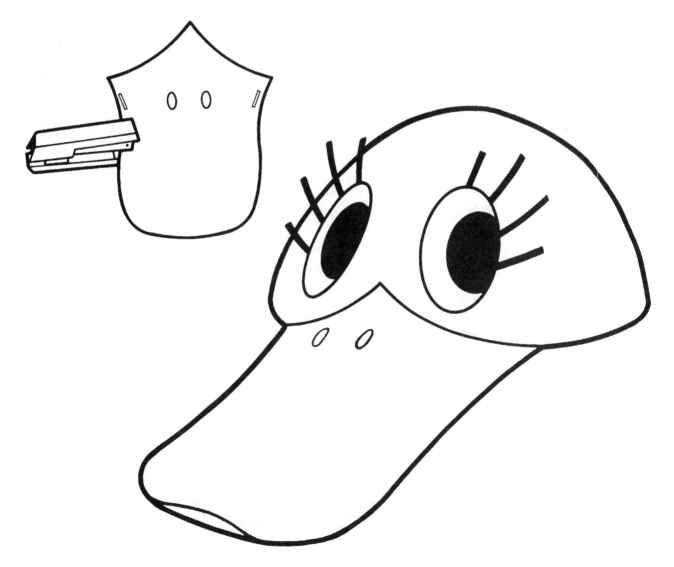

Ducks *(cont.)*

Duck Bill Pattern

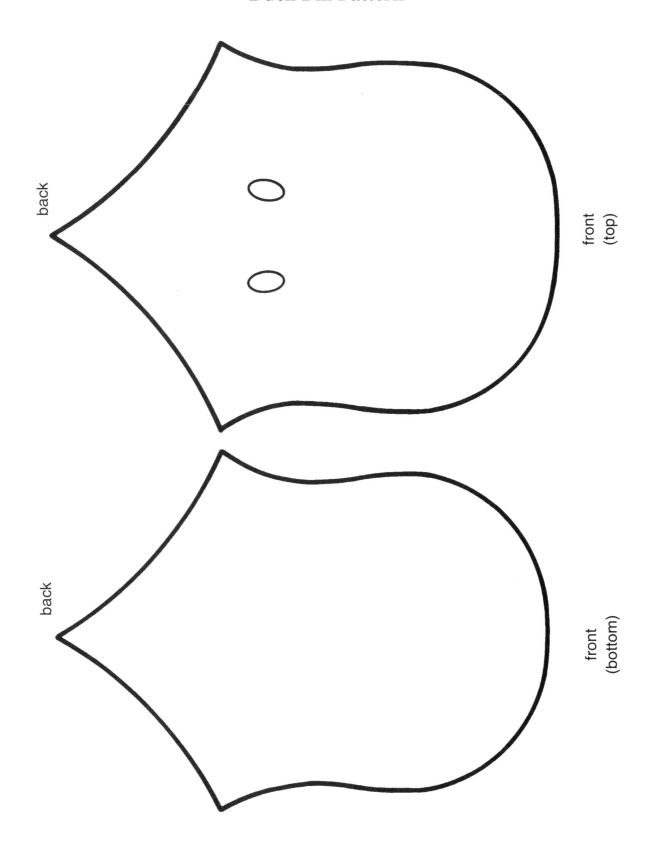

Pigs

For each pig, you will need the following items:

1. one pink basic headpiece
2. a pair of pink ears
3. a snout
4. a pair of eyes
5. a curly tail
6. an optional baseball cap
7. pink T-shirt or sweatshirt

From construction paper, cut a circle on a spiral line. Pull the spiral out and pin it to the back of the shirt so it hangs outward a bit.

curly tail

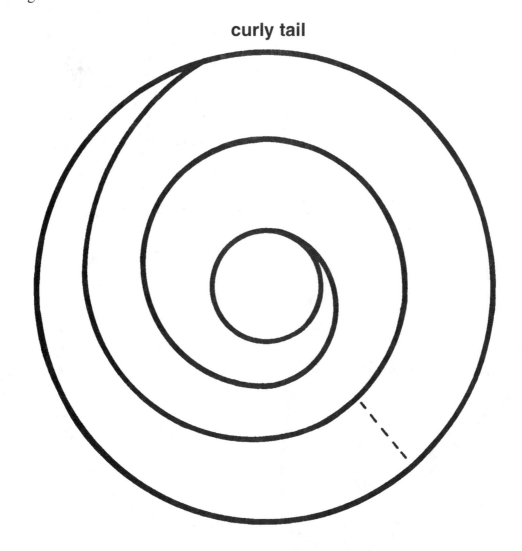

Pigs *(cont.)*

Pig's Snout

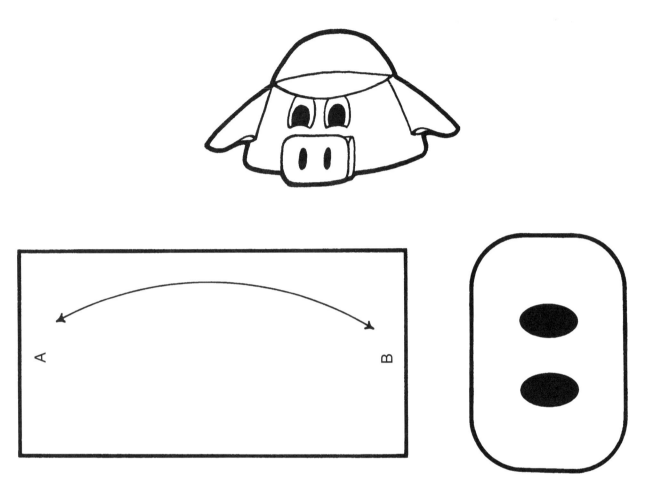

1. Cut rectangular and oval pieces from pink construction paper.

2. Outline the oval and nostrils with a black felt marker.

3. Roll A to B, forming a cylinder, and staple the ends together.

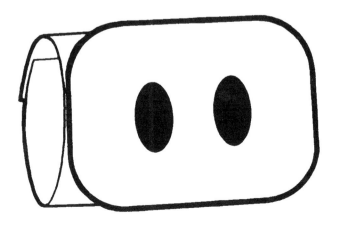

4. Cut and attach the oval snout to the cylinder, and glue this to the bottom edge of the headpiece.

Pigs *(cont.)*

Pig's Ears

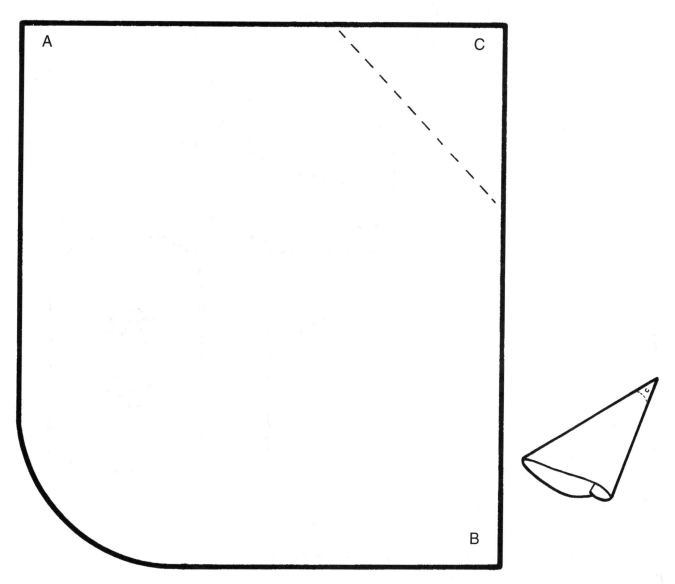

1. Cut two ears from pink construction paper.

2. Roll each ear, cone-like, bringing A to B, and staple the ends together.

3. Make two-inch (5 cm) slits on each side of the headpiece.

4. Insert the C end into the slit. Fold the C end and secure it to the inside of the headpiece.

5. See the illustration on page 26.

Pigs *(cont.)*

Pig's Ears *(cont.)*

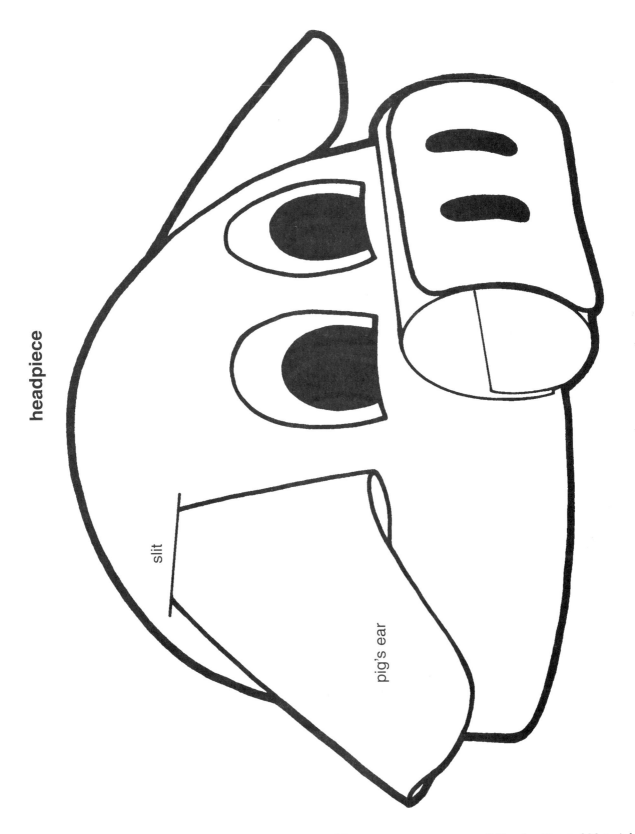

Pigs *(cont.)*

Baseball Cap

1. Cut the pattern shown on page 28 out of folded tagboard. Open it to form a circle. Use the circle as a pattern to cut a baseball cap from colored construction paper.

2. Form the cap from the circle, using the directions for a basic headpiece.

3. Cut and attach the visor. Put the cap on the pig.

visor for baseball cap

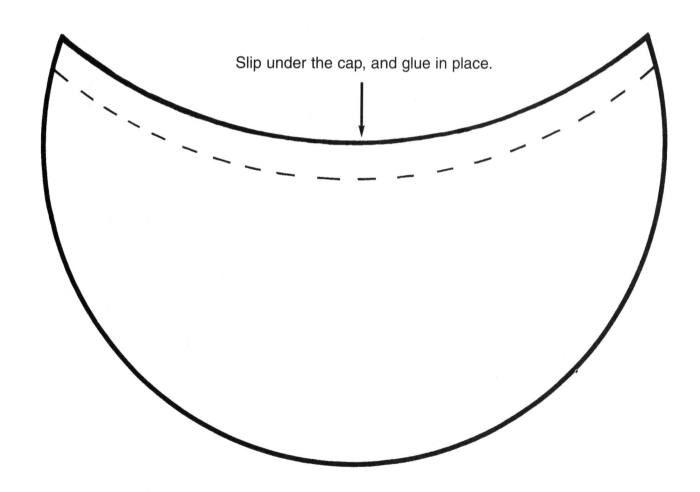

Slip under the cap, and glue in place.

Pigs *(cont.)*

Baseball Cap *(cont.)*

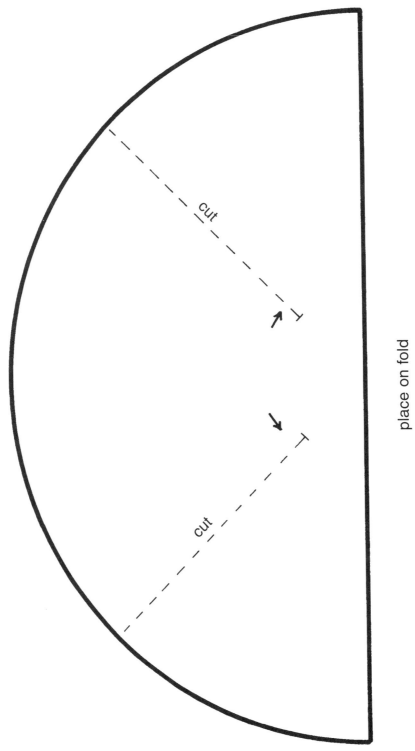

Cows

This cow pattern is for a black and white Holstein cow. Use the same directions with appropriate colors for any other cow being portrayed.

Assembly

1. Make the headpiece from white construction paper and paint black blotches on it.

2. Make two ears from black construction paper (see pattern on page 30). Paint the insides of the ears pink. Insert the ends of the ears into slits made on the sides of the headpiece. Secure them with tape.

Cows *(cont.)*

Assembly *(cont.)*

3. Make the snout white and the nostrils pink (see diagram on page 31).

4. Make large eyes with long lashes (page 20).

5. Paper or silk flowers may be added on the top of the cow's head, near its ear.

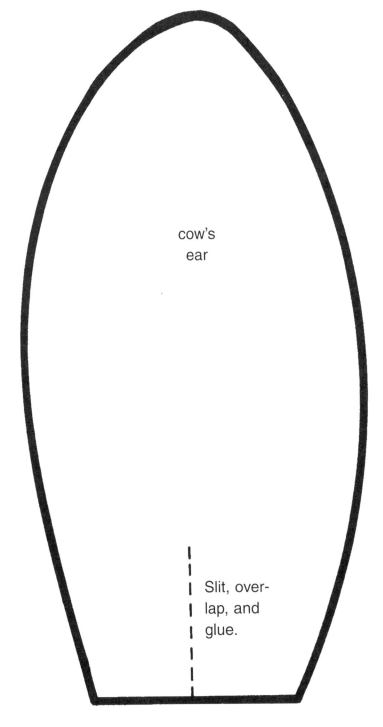

cow's
ear

Slit, over-
lap, and
glue.

Cows *(cont.)*

Cow's Snout

1. Cut the rectangle from white construction paper.

2. Roll end to end to form a cylinder and then staple ends.

3. Cut the oval for the nostrils from pink construction paper.

4. Use a black felt marker to outline oval and nostrils.

5. Glue the nostrils to the snout (cylinder).

6. Attach at the bottom of the cow's face.

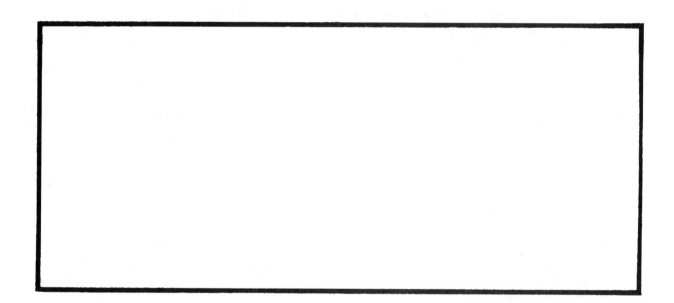

Goats

(Three Billy Goats Gruff)

1. Make three goat costumes.

2. Troll—Use a rubber Halloween mask that is scary or funny but NOT gruesome!

3. Make many background characters for the meadow—flowers, birds, bees, butterflies, plants, etc.

4. Make a bridge using a low table and stepping blocks for stairs. Paint a cardboard front for the bridge.

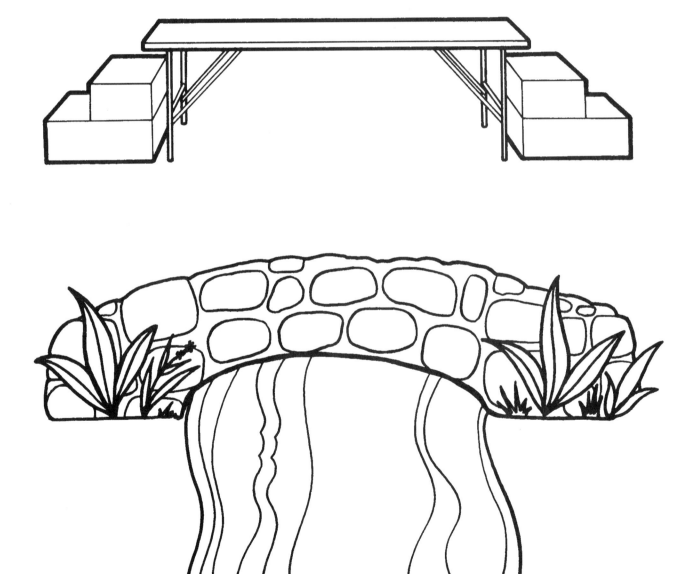

Goats *(cont.)*

For each goat, make the following items:

1. one basic headpiece from construction paper in the color of your choice (gray, brown, tan, black, or white)

2. one pair of ears (See pattern on page 35.)

3. one beard (See pattern on page 36.)

4. one pair of horns (see pattern on page 36.)

5. one pair of eyes

6. one pink or black circle for a nose

7. one yoke or collar (See pattern on 37.)

Note: Children are to wear sweats in matching colors.

Goats *(cont.)*

Assembly

1. Attach the ears to the headpiece.

2. Paint irregular island shapes on the headpiece and yoke (black or gray on white, dark brown or black on tan, white or gray on black, black or gray on white).

3. Glue on eyes (page 20) and a small black circle for the nose.

4. Lace rubber band for straps and attach them to the headpiece with brass paper fasteners.

5. Cut a triangular beard from construction paper. Drape it over the rubber band strap at the chin point and staple it in place. Glue cotton over the beard piece.

6. Cut horns and attach them to the headpiece.

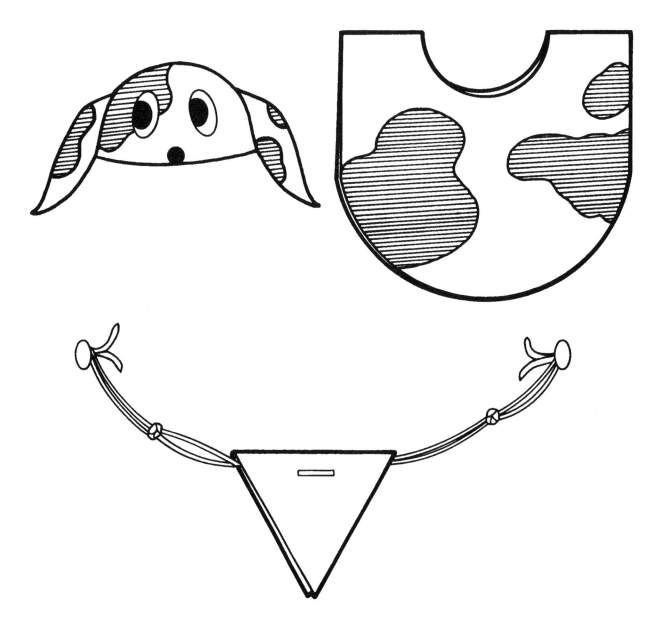

Goats *(cont.)*

Goat Ears

(also to be used for sheep)

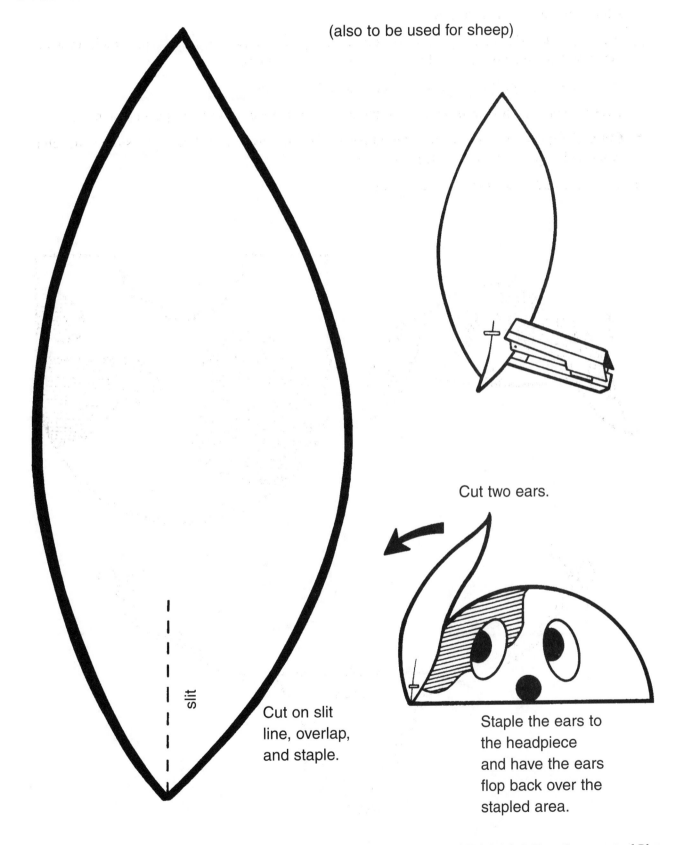

slit

Cut on slit line, overlap, and staple.

Cut two ears.

Staple the ears to the headpiece and have the ears flop back over the stapled area.

Goats *(cont.)*

Goat Beards

Cut on the fold. Drape over the rubber band strap. Staple in place and glue cotton over the beard shape.

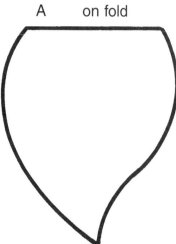

A   on fold

B   on fold

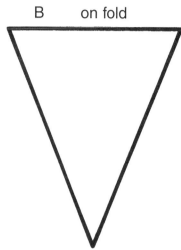

Goat Horns

Cut with the tip of the horn on a fold of white construction paper. The horns may be lengthened if desired. Make two slits at the top of the headpiece. Insert the horns from under the headpiece. Bend the tabs and glue or tape them to the underside of the headpiece.

on fold

tab

tape

Goat Horns

Goats *(cont.)*

Yoke or Collar

To make a pattern, cut from tagboard on the fold and then open it to use as a pattern for construction paper yokes.

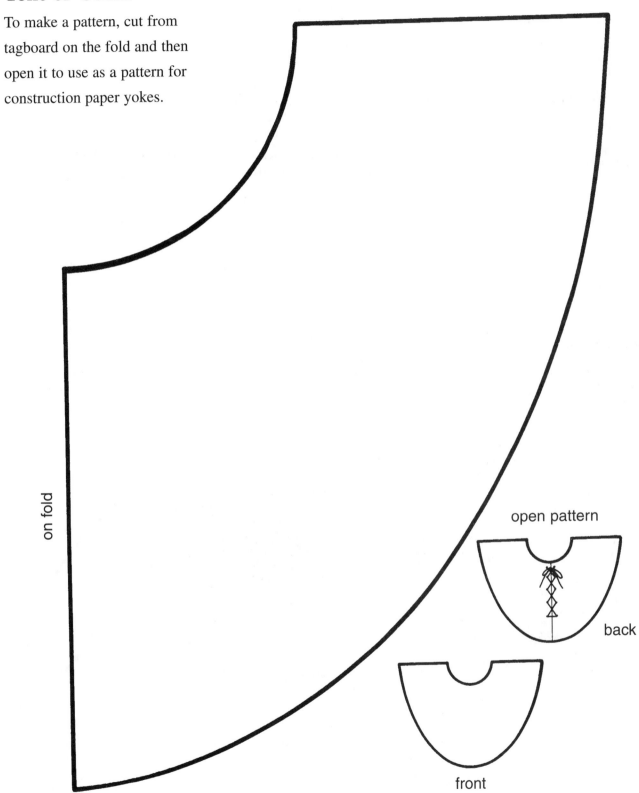

on fold

open pattern

back

front

Sheep

For each sheep or lamb, you will need the following items:

1. one basic headpiece from white or black construction paper

2. one pair of ears, using the goat ear pattern on page 35

3. one pair of large expressive eyes on page 20

4. a pink circle for the nose

5. one yoke or collar, using the pattern from page 37

6. lots of fluffy cotton to glue around the face, top, and back of the headpiece and on the front and back of the yoke (If the sheep or lamb is to be black, lightly spray the cotton with black paint.)

7. white or black sweats for the children to wear, depending on the chosen color

Birds

Birds of bright blue, red, and yellow add much to a forest, meadow, or garden background.

For each bird, you will need the following items:

1. one basic headpiece from construction paper in the color of your choice
2. one pair of eyes
3. one pair of wings
4. one body vest
5. one beak (See pattern on page 40.)

Assembly

Follow the basic directions for the hen and the duck.

Birds *(cont.)*

Bird's Beak

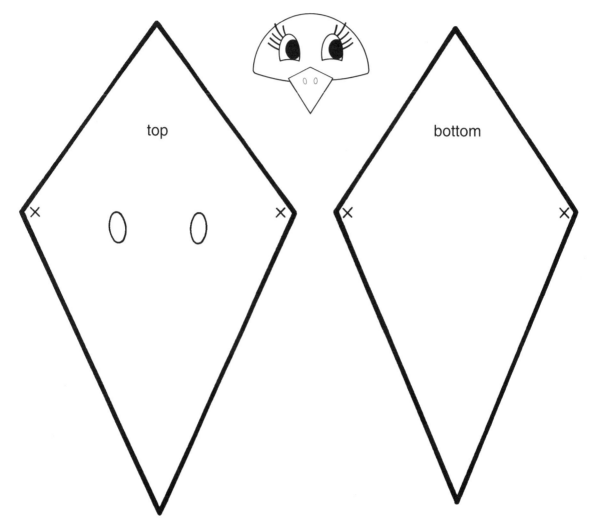

1. Cut one top and one bottom from bright yellow construction paper.

2. Match the ends of the top over the bottom and staple the pieces together where the X's are. The top is slightly larger, so it should show a slight pucker.

3. Insert the bottom front of the headpiece between the two layers (as was done with the duck's bill) and then staple it in place.

Birds *(cont.)*

Crow's Beak

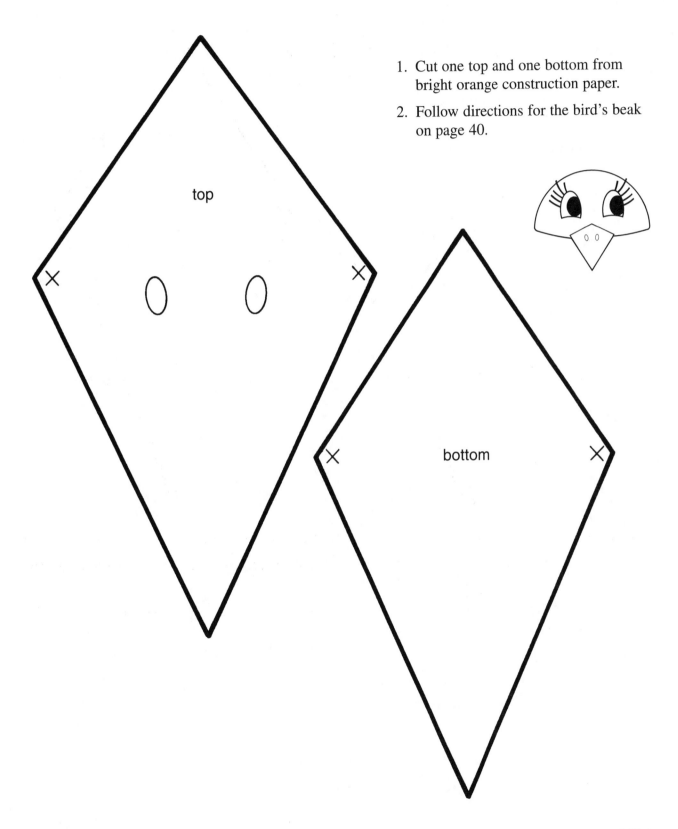

1. Cut one top and one bottom from bright orange construction paper.

2. Follow directions for the bird's beak on page 40.

Birds *(cont.)*

Mardi Gras Birds

Mardi Gras birds add splash to your background. Most children love to use feathers, sequins, stones, beads, and foil to embellish their costumes.

Cut the pattern on page 43 on a fold of dark or bright construction paper (blacks, deep purples, etc.). Have the children create their own beautiful birds.

Use the basic wing patterns for these birds.

(Construction paper masks may need to be reinforced with a tagboard backing. This costume is really fun—let the kids' imaginations run riot!)

Birds *(cont.)*

Mardi Gras Bird Mask

on fold

Birds *(cont.)*

Owl Mask

For the owl mask, you will need the following items:

1. a yellow beak, following the pattern and directions for the bird beak on page 40

2. two large circles of white construction paper to serve as eye backgrounds

3. white feathers to glue around the eye circles (if available)

4. a basic body vest of gray as shown on pages 10–12

5. mask pattern on folded tagboard as shown on page 45 (Unfold this and use it as a base on which to glue gray construction paper, white eye circles, yellow beak, and feathers.)

Birds *(cont.)*

Owl Mask *(cont.)*

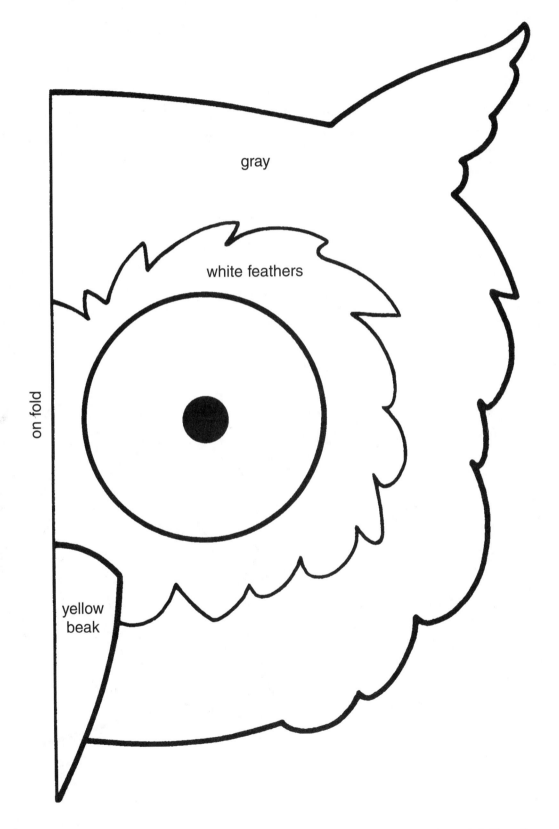

gray

white feathers

on fold

yellow
beak

Cats

1. Make cats by using the basic headpieces (pages 8 and 9) in the colors of your choice.

2. Matching body vests are optional. If children are wearing leotards and tights of the same color as their headpieces, you will not need body vests.

Assembly

1. Make the headpieces.

2. Cut two ears (construction paper) from the ear pattern below. Paint the inside of the ears with pink paint.

3. Make a slit at the base of the ear, overlap slightly, and glue. The overlap will give the ear a three-dimensional effect.

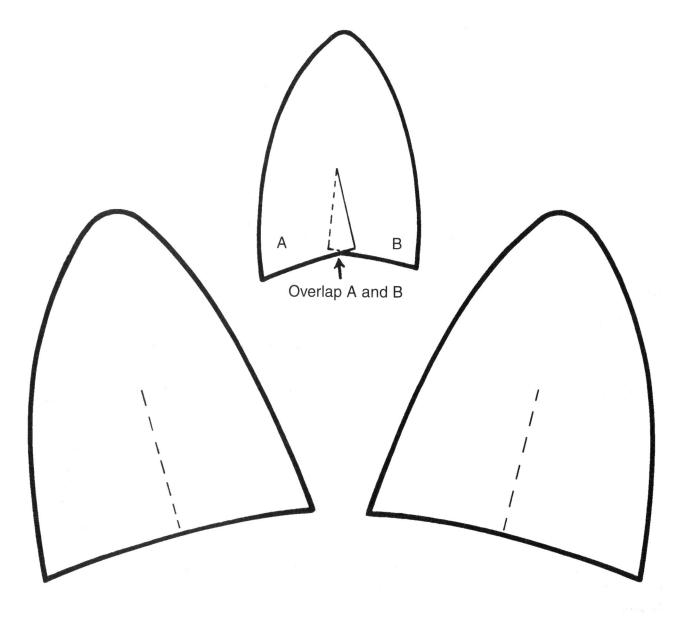

A   B

Overlap A and B

Cats *(cont.)*

Faces

1. Make a pair of eyes from white construction paper. Paint the pupils and irises in bright colors—greens, yellows, blues. Outline them in black.

2. Make a triangle from pink construction paper for the nose.

3. Make long black whiskers from black pipe cleaners.

Tails

1. Cut two long strips of construction paper to the length desired for the tail.

2. Use a medium-gauge length of floral wiring to give the tail form and lift. Place the wire between the two tail strips and glue.

3. Attach to the back of the body vest or leotard, high enough to easily clear the ground.

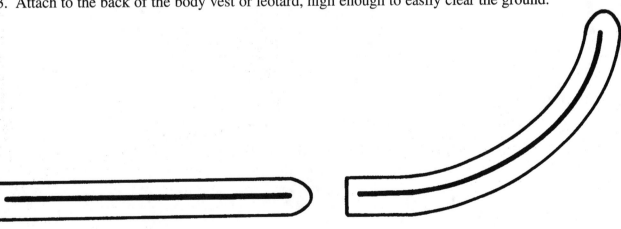

Raccoons

1. Cut the raccoon mask (page 49) on a fold of gray construction paper.

2. Outline the mask in black. Paint around the eyes with black paint for the "masked bandit" look.

3. Softly color in shades of white and soft black in the direction of hair growth.

4. Make slits at the ear where they are marked on the pattern.

5. Fold the nose two times, accordion style. Staple just a bit of the innermost fold to the mask to give the nose a lift.

6. Cut a black circle and glue it to the tip of the nose.

7. Attach brass paper fasteners to the sides of the mask, and use rubber band lacings for expandable straps.

8. See page 52 for the tail directions.

Raccoons *(cont.)*

Raccoon Mask

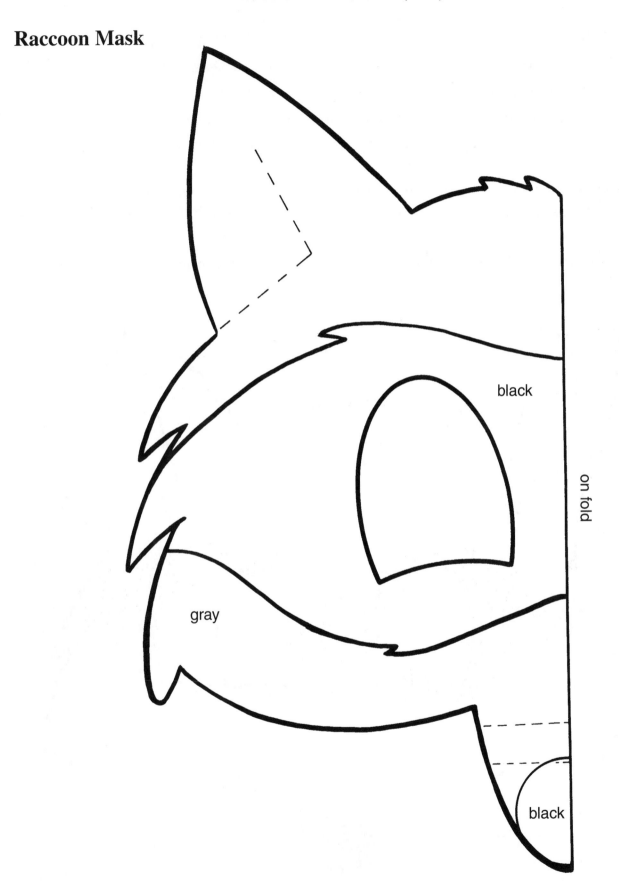

gray

black

on fold

black

Foxes

Fox Mask

1. Cut the fox mask pattern (page 51) on a fold of tan construction paper.

2. Outline the mask in red or brown with paint or markers. Outline the eyes.

3. Softly color in shades of red and brown in the direction of hair growth.

4. Make slits at the ear where shown on the pattern. Fold the outer edge over and staple to form the ear.

5. Fold the nose two times, accordion style. Staple just a bit of the innermost fold to the mask to give the nose a lift.

6. Cut a black circle and glue it to the tip of the nose.

7. Attach brass paper fasteners to the sides of the mask and use rubber band lacings for expandable straps.

8. See pages 52 for tail directions.

Foxes *(cont.)*

Fox Mask *(cont.)*

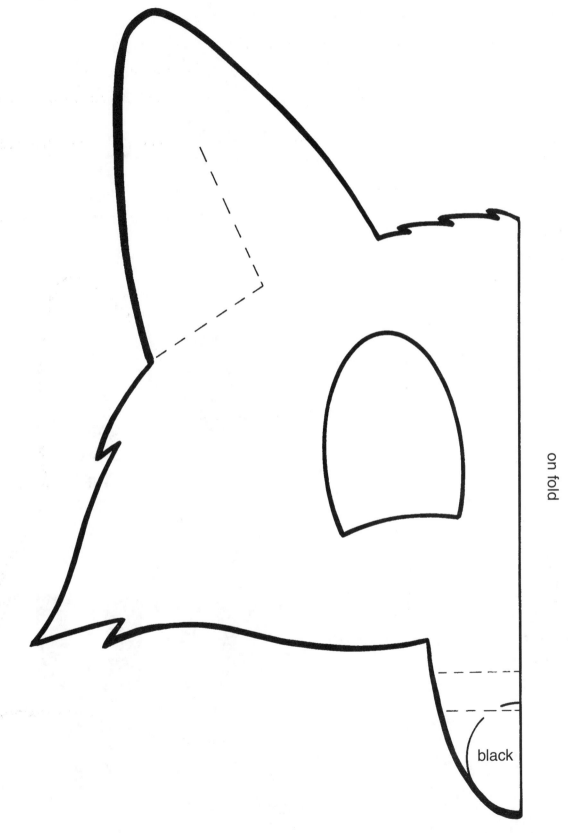

on fold

black

Foxes *(cont.)*

Body Vests and Tails (for fox, raccoon, and skunk)

Fox

1. Make a body vest (pages 10–12). Shade in softly with browns and reds.

2. Make a bushy tail and attach to the back.

 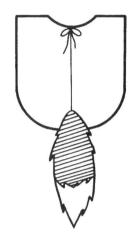

Raccoon

1. Make a body vest (pages 10–12).

2. Make a ringed tail and attach to the back.

Skunk

1. Make a body vest (pages 10–12). Paint a wide white stripe on the back of the vest.

2. Make a black tail with a centered white stripe. Attach it to the back.

Skunks

Directions for two skunk masks (A and B) follow. Use whichever one you wish.

Mask A

1. Cut the mask on page 54 on a fold of black construction paper.

2. Paint a white stripe on the face—narrow above the nose, widening as it reaches the top.

3. Follow the directions from the raccoon pages (pages 48 and 49).

4. End with a pink tip for the nose.

Skunks *(cont.)*

Skunk Mask

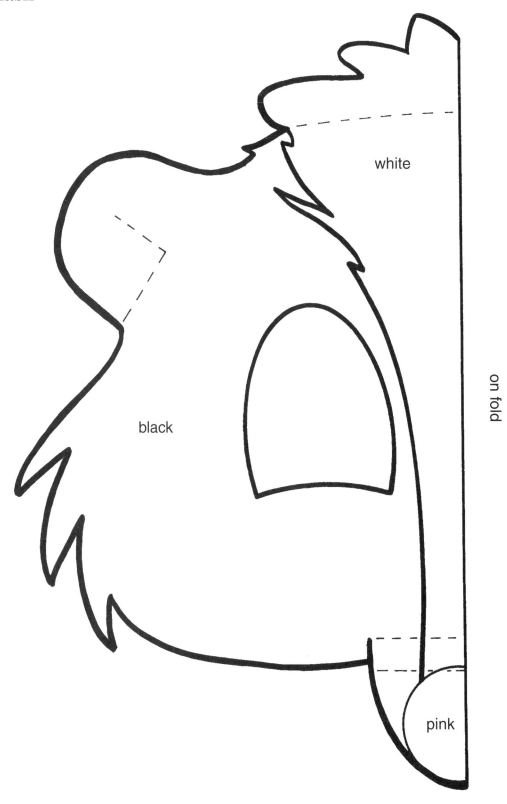

white

black

on fold

pink

Skunks *(cont.)*

Mask B

1. Cut the mask on page 54 on a fold of black construction paper.

2. Follow the directions for the raccoon mask (pages 48 and 49) to form the ears and nose.

3. Cut the following pieces (pages 55 and 56) from white construction paper and put them together to simulate a white stripe on the center of the mask.

1. Cut out A.

2. Cut out C and cut in on lines of C.

3. Slightly curl up the fringed edges of C.

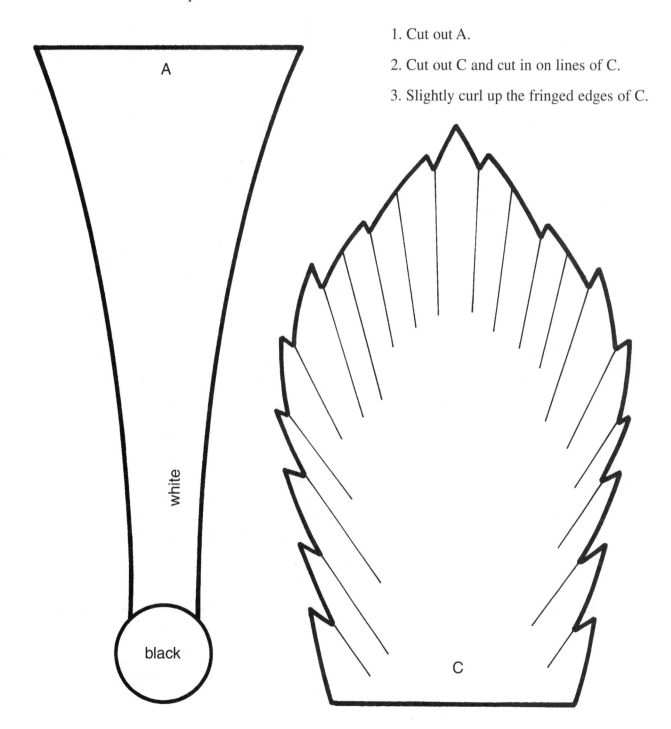

Skunks *(cont.)*

Mask B *(cont.)*

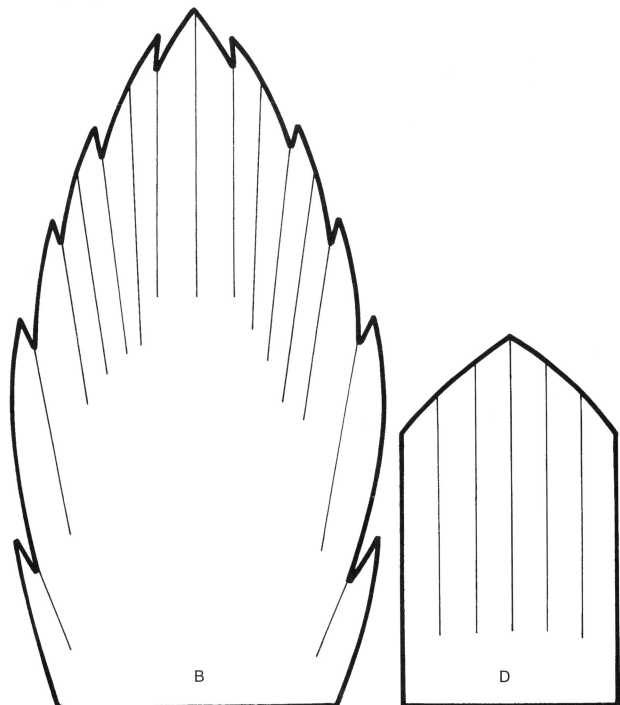

1. Cut out B and cut in on lines of B.

2. Slightly curl up the fringed edges of B.

3. Cut out D and cut in on lines of D.

4. Slightly curl up the fringed edges of D.

Skunks *(cont.)*

Mask B *(cont.)*

1. After cutting white pieces A, B, C, and D on pages 55 and 56, glue piece A (the long narrow piece with the nose tip) in the center of the mask from the nose upward.

2. Cut and curl the edges of B (the largest white piece) and glue from one inch (2.5 cm) behind the mask over and down toward the nose.

3. C goes over B, starting again from behind the mask.

4. End with D (the smallest piece). A layered, curled look should be achieved.

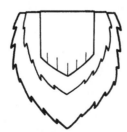

5. Cut a black circle for the tip of the nose.

Beavers

1. Make a basic headpiece (pages 8 and 9) of brown construction paper.

2. Use basic body vest of brown (pages 10–12).

3. Add eyes and nose of black construction paper and glue onto headpiece as shown.

4. Use white construction paper to form teeth. Outline the teeth with a marker and staple them to the bottom of the headpiece.

5. Cut out ear patterns shown below. Cut along the slits as shown, overlap to give dimension, and glue or tape the ears to the headpiece.

6. Make a tail from the pattern below in brown construction paper, drawing thick black lines as shown with a thick-tipped marker.

Rabbits

1. Make a basic headpiece (pages 8 and 9) of white or brown construction paper.

2. Make a basic body vest (pages 10–12) of the same color as the headpiece.

3. Use a large white pompon as a tail to attach to the back of the body vest (or to leotards if they are worn) with tape.

4. Make a pair of expressive eyes (page 20) to glue on the headpiece, as shown. Add eyelashes if desired.

5. Make slits toward back of headpiece to insert ears of white or brown as shown in illustration. Color the center of the ears pink. See page 60 for ear pattern.

Rabbits *(cont.)*

Rabbit Ears

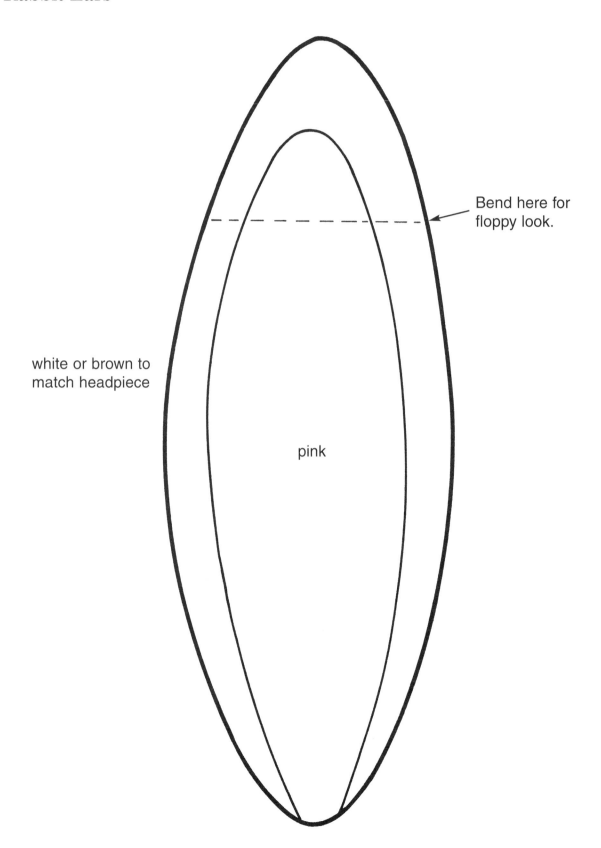

Bend here for
floppy look.

white or brown to
match headpiece

pink

Bears

Three Bears Patterns

The adaptation of *Goldilocks and the Three Bears* makes use of a look somewhat different from that achieved solely by cap headpieces. A form of over-the-face mask is used for the bears, skunks, raccoons, and foxes. However, concerns for visibility and audibility (for both cast and audience) require that the eye openings be large and that the mouth areas be left uncovered. The other forest plants and animals—birds, rabbits, bees, and flowers—will use the regular cap headpieces.

Bear Patterns

See the patterns on pages 62 and 63 for the masks to create Papa Bear, Mama Bear, and Baby Bear on folded construction paper, according to the directions given below. You may wish to enlarge the patterns a bit if the size of your students requires it.

1. Cut the bear patterns from brown, black, or tan construction paper.

2. Cut slits at the ears. Tuck the outer ends under the inner ends and staple to give the ears form.

3. Fold the snout accordion style, stapling the innermost pleat to the mask. Adjust as needed to form the snout.

4. Cut black circles for the tips of Mama and Papa Bear's noses.

5. Insert brass paper fasteners at the sides of the masks.

6. Attach rubber band lacings to the paper fasteners for an expandable strap to hold the mask on the student's face.

7. Students may wear sweat tops and bottoms the color of the bears, or they may wear basic body vests made of the same color.

8. Mama Bear may wear a flower and an apron.

Bears *(cont.)*

Bear Patterns *(cont.)*

Papa Bear and **Mama Bear**

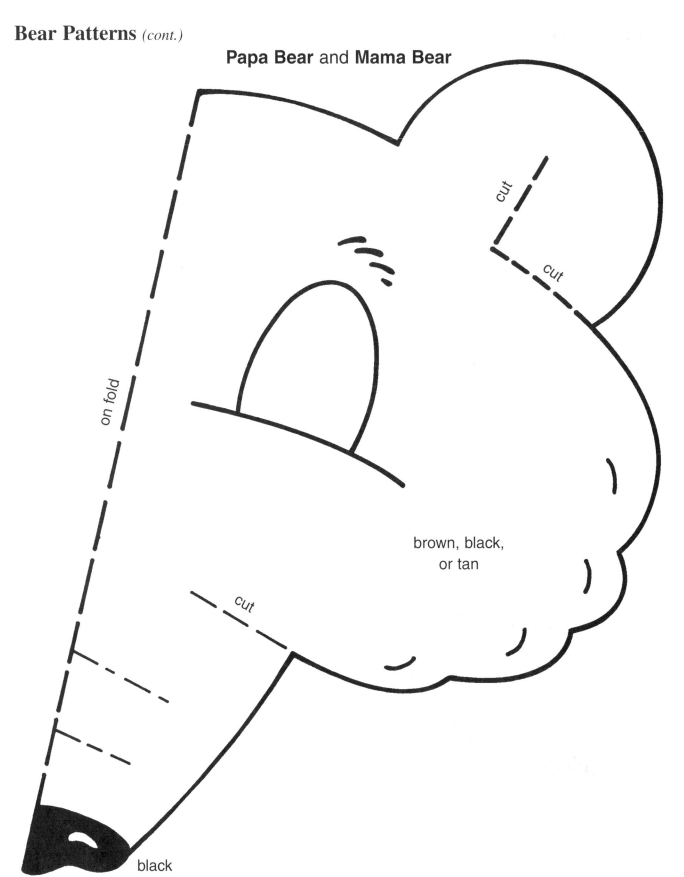

cut

cut

on fold

cut

brown, black,
or tan

cut

black

Bears *(cont.)*

Bear Patterns *(cont.)*

Baby Bear

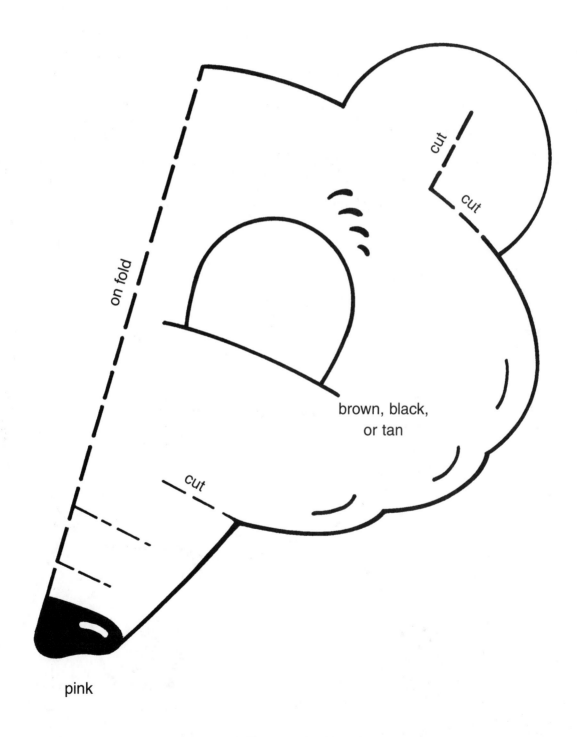

Honeybees

For each honeybee, you will need the following items:

1. one black basic headpiece (pages 8 and 9)

2. one yellow basic body vest (pages 10–12)

3. white tissue paper for wings

4. one long—at least 12" (30 cm)—black pipe cleaner or chenille stick

Assembly

Head

1. Make a basic headpiece from black construction paper.

2. Punch or poke two holes about two inches (5 cm) apart on the top of the headpiece.

3. Insert the black pipe cleaner down through one hole and up through the other. Even the pipe cleaner ends so that the antennae are the same length. Bend the tips forward.

4. Make big buggy eyes to place on the headpiece.

Honeybees *(cont.)*

Body

1. Make a yellow body vest (pages 10–12).

2. Make wide black stripes on front and back of the body vest, using black paint or black construction paper strips.

3. Using two large sheets of white tissue paper per wing, round off the corners and gather each at the center.

4. Cut down the back of the body vest. Punch two holes at the top for ties. Attach the wings.

5. Children should wear black leotards and tights.

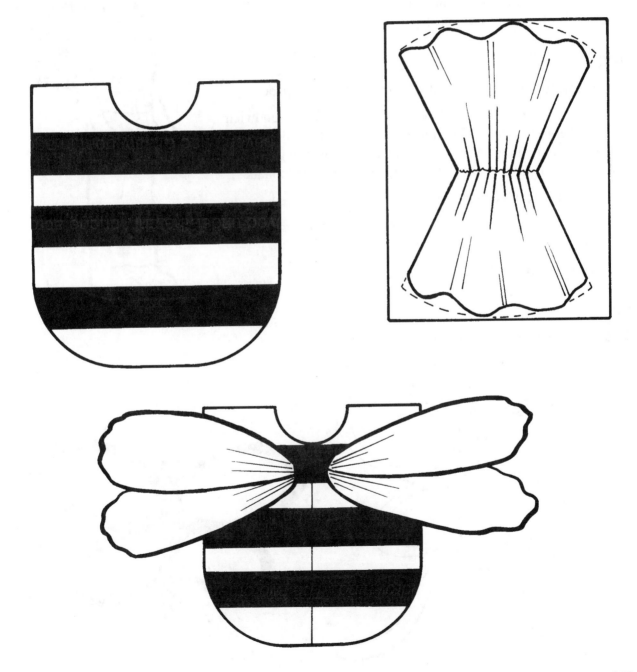

Butterflies

Assembly

Head

1. Make a basic headpiece (pages 8 and 9) from black construction paper.

2. Make one pair of eyes (page 20).

3. Loop one pipe cleaner or chenille stick through the headpiece for antennae as described on page 64.

4. Attach two small Styrofoam balls glittered with silver or gold to the ends of the pipe cleaner.

Wings

1. Cut a wing frame from doubled black construction paper.

2. Colored tissue paper or cellophane should be glued, sandwich style, between the doubled frame where areas have been cut open. Plain butterflies may be created later by taping tan wrapping paper over the colored tissue paper or cellophane.

3. Open areas may be made simple or intricate as desired.

4. Attach the wings at the top with a sturdy safety pin and ribbon sash looped through holes at the waist.

5. Enlarge pattern.

Body

1. Make a basic body vest of black or dark bright color.

2. Children should wear black leotards and tights.

Butterflies *(cont.)*

Wing Pattern

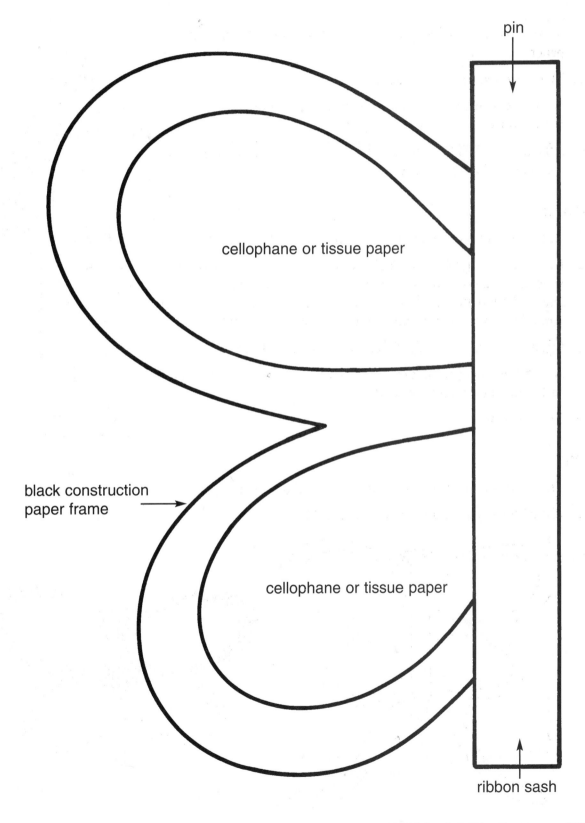

pin

cellophane or tissue paper

black construction
paper frame

cellophane or tissue paper

ribbon sash

Flowers

1. Trace and cut eight construction or butcher paper petals for each flower.

2. Trace and cut eight coordinating or contrasting colored tissue paper petals for each flower.

3. Make a basic headpiece (pages 8 and 9) using the color you have chosen for the center of your flower (yellow, brown, orange, etc.).

4. Assemble and staple petals around the bottom edge of the headpiece.

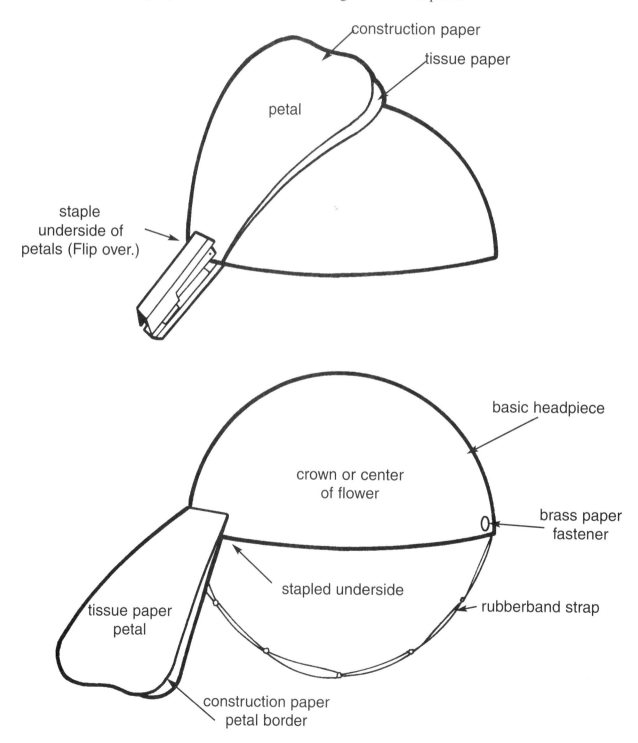

construction paper

tissue paper

petal

staple underside of petals (Flip over.)

basic headpiece

crown or center of flower

brass paper fastener

stapled underside

rubberband strap

tissue paper petal

construction paper petal border

Flowers *(cont.)*

Flower Petal Pattern

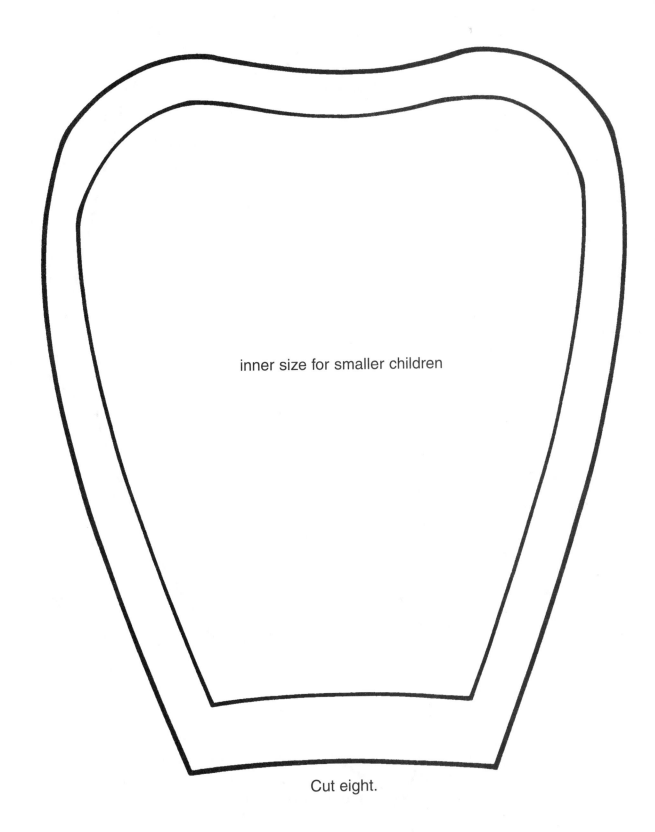

inner size for smaller children

Cut eight.

Flowers *(cont.)*

Flower Collar Pattern

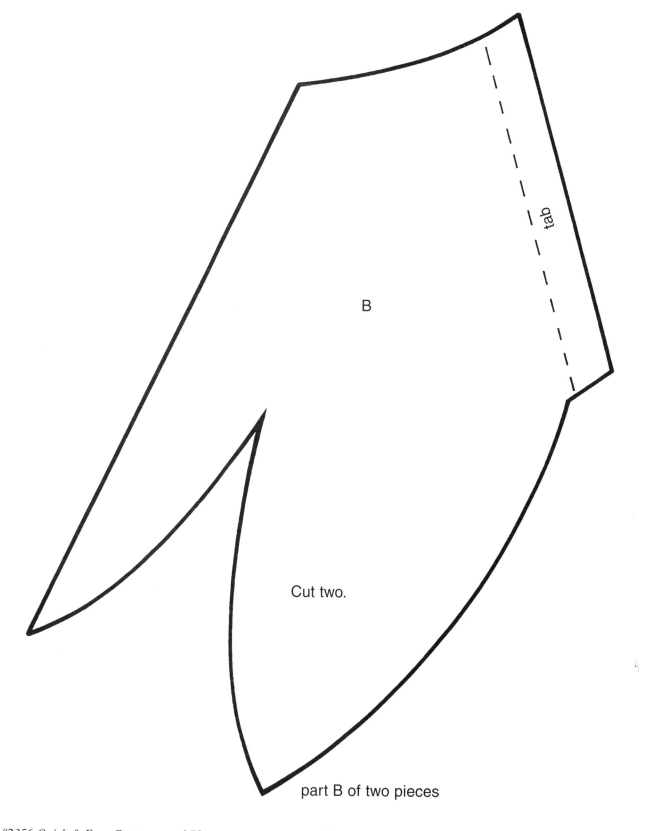

B

tab

Cut two.

part B of two pieces

Flowers *(cont.)*

Flower Collar Pattern *(cont.)*

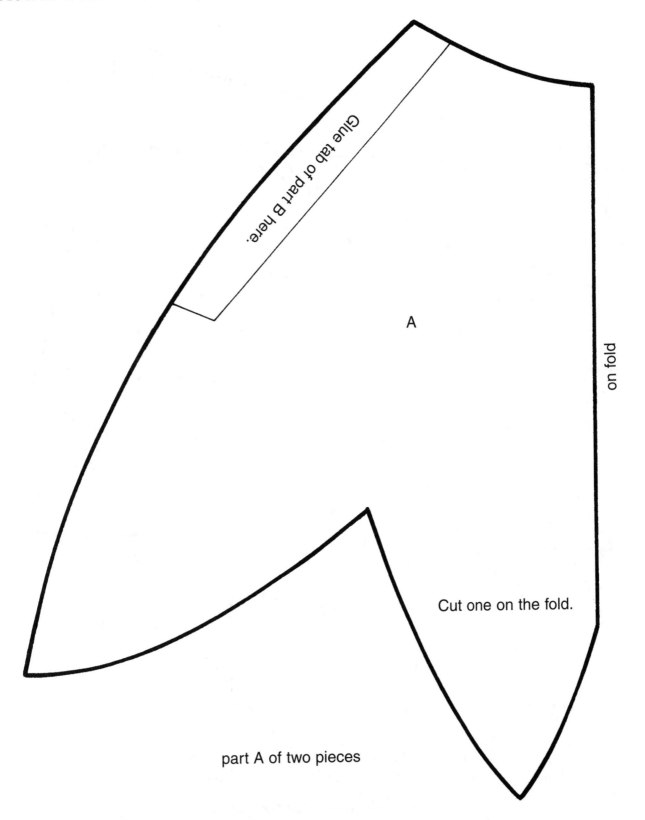

Glue tab of part B here.

A

on fold

Cut one on the fold.

part A of two pieces

Flowers *(cont.)*

Assemble Pattern for Collar

1. Cut A on fold of tagboard and open up.

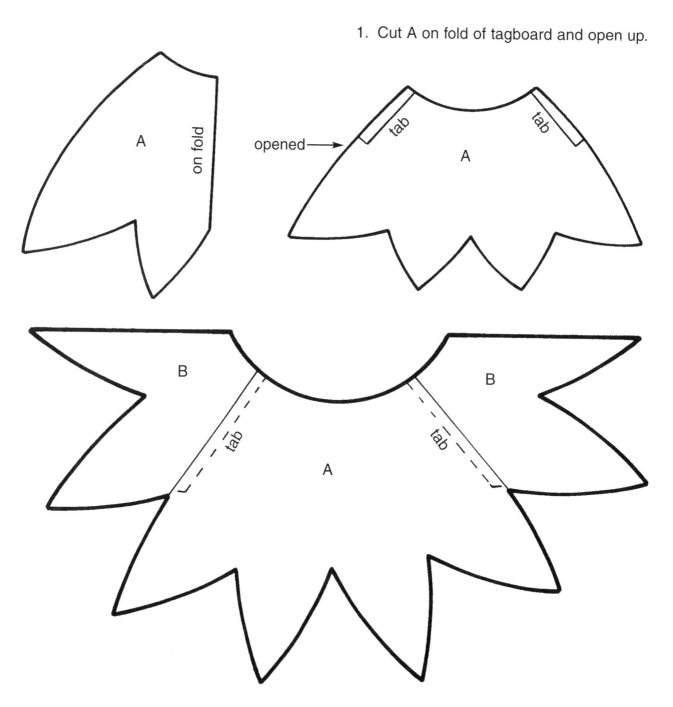

2. Cut two pieces of B out of tagboard. Glue tabs of B over tab marks on A to form collar pattern.

3. To make flower collars, see page 73.

Flowers *(cont.)*

Flower Collars

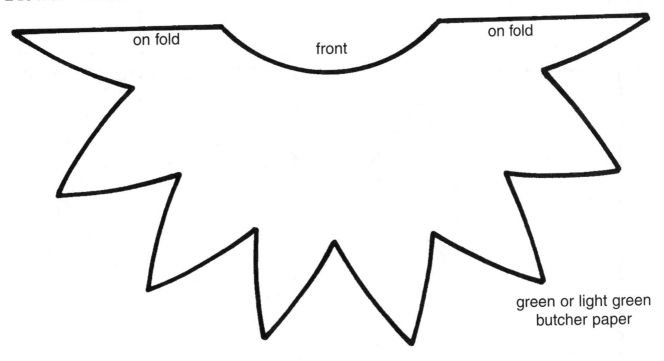

1. Place collar pattern you assembled from pieces A and B on folded butcher paper (green or light green). Make sure that the top (shoulder) of the pattern is on the fold. Cut to form the front and back.

2. Cut down the center of the back. Punch two holes and reinforce the area around the holes.

3. Insert ties in the holes (yarn or twine).

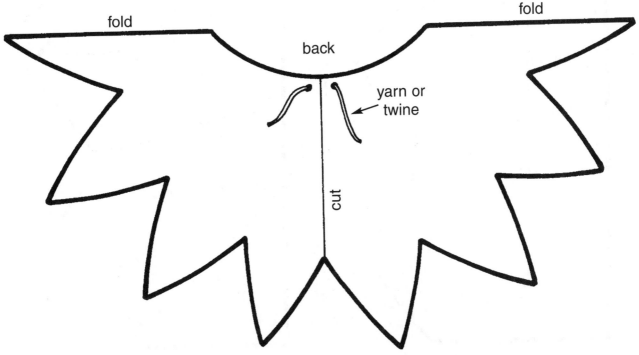

Crown

Reproduce onto heavy paper. Make as many pieces as needed to fit a child's head. Tape pieces together to create a crown.

Little Red Hen

Cast

Narrator _____ (nice clothes)

Little Red Hen _____ (costume: pages 17–19)

Chicks _____ (costume: pages 17–19)

Cat _____ (costume: pages 46 and 47)

Pig _____ (costume: pages 23–28)

Duck _____ (costume: pages 20–22)

Props: seed, several stalks of wheat, large piece of brown paper or fabric for mud puddle, eggs, table, nest for duck to sit on, large circular piece of blue butcher paper (or fabric) for duck pond, pig's feed trough, fence post, ball of yarn, wheelbarrow, spade, kitchen timer, two potholders, one empty cake pan, mixing bowl, mixing spoon, bag of flour, measuring cup with water in it, one cake pan with a baked cake in it

Setting: barnyard *(Little Red Hen's chicks are **always** with her, following her throughout the play.)*

Little Red Hen *(cont.)*

Narrator: One morning Little Red Hen was pecking for food when she discovered something.

Little Red Hen: What's this? *(Bends over to pick a grain of wheat up from the ground and holds it up for all to see as her chicks crowd around her.)* Why, it's a grain of wheat! I will plant it right away! *(She bustles off to plant the wheat with the chicks trailing behind her.)*

Narrator: On her way to plant the grain of wheat, the Little Red Hen came across her friend Duck swimming in the pond. *(Duck enters from the right and pantomimes swimming.)*

Little Red Hen: Hi there, Duck! Will you help me plant this grain of wheat?

Duck: No. I am too busy swimming!
(Cat enters from the right and comes up to Little Red Hen.)

Little Red Hen: Hi there, Cat! Will you help me plant this grain of wheat?

Cat: No. I am too busy looking for mice! *(Little Red Hen continues across the stage. Pig enters from the right and rolls on the ground in delight.)*

Little Red Hen: Hi there, Pig! Will you help me plant this grain of wheat?

Pig: No. I am too busy rolling in this lovely mud puddle!

Little Red Hen: *(to chicks)* Then I will plant it myself.

Narrator: And she did. *(Little Red Hen pantomimes digging a hole and planting the seed and covering it up with dirt.)* Time passed, and soon it was midsummer. The wheat grew ripe, and Little Red Hen went back to her friends in the barnyard.

Little Red Hen: Duck, will you help me harvest the wheat?

Duck: No. I am too busy sitting on my eggs!

Little Red Hen: Cat, will you help me harvest the wheat?

Little Red Hen *(cont.)*

Cat: No. I am too busy licking my fur! *(Cat licks fur.)*

Little Red Hen: Pig, will you help me harvest the wheat?

Pig: No. I am too busy eating! *(Pig sticks head back into feed trough.)*

Little Red Hen: *(to chicks)* Then I will harvest it myself.

Narrator: And she did. *(Little Red Hen pulls up wheat by its roots, grunting and straining with the effort. She puts the wheat into a wheelbarrow.)*

Little Red Hen: *(to chicks)* Now I need to take this to the mill to be ground into flour. *(She pushes the wheelbarrow across stage toward the barnyard.)*

Narrator: Little Red Hen saw her friends in the barnyard.

Little Red Hen: Duck, will you help me take the wheat to the mill so it can be ground into flour?

Duck: No. I am too busy tending my ducklings!

Little Red Hen: Cat, will you help me take the wheat to the mill so it can be ground into flour?

Cat: No. I am too busy scratching this terrific fence post! *(Cat scratches post.)*

Little Red Hen: Pig, will you help me take the wheat to the mill so it can be ground into flour?

Pig: No. I am too busy digesting my lunch! *(Pig rubs tummy and sighs happily.)*

Little Red Hen: *(to chicks)* Then I will take it to the mill myself!

Narrator: And she did. *(Little Red Hen pushes wheelbarrow across the stage away from the barnyard, exerting herself because of the weight she's pushing. Little Red Hen exits stage.)* As soon as the miller had ground the wheat into flour, Little Red Hen put it back into her wheelbarrow and went home. *(Little Red Hen enters stage, pushing wheelbarrow, stopping at the barnyard.)*

Little Red Hen: Duck, will you help me make this flour into a cake?

Little Red Hen (cont.)

Duck: No. I am too busy resting. The sun is hot today!

Little Red Hen: Cat, will you help me make this flour into a cake?

Cat: No. I am too busy playing with this wonderful ball of yarn! *(Cat bats around a ball of yarn and looks thrilled with it.)*

Little Red Hen: Pig, will you help me make this flour into cake?

Pig: No. I am too busy sunning myself! *(Pig snorts happily and rolls back over onto his back to sun himself.)*

Little Red Hen: *(to chicks)* Then I will make a cake myself!

Narrator: And she did. *(Little Red Hen pantomimes mixing in a bowl and putting a pan into an oven offstage.)* Soon the delicious smell of baking cake spread throughout the barnyard. The duck, the cat, and the pig followed their noses to Little Red Hen's kitchen. *(They stand around, waiting for the cake to come out of the oven. A timer buzzes offstage.)* When the cake was ready, Little Red Hen took it from the oven. *(She removes cake from the "oven" offstage and carefully carries it onstage, using pot holders.)*

Little Red Hen: Who will help me eat this cake?

Duck, Cat, and Pig: *(all together)* I will! *(All three rush forward eagerly, reaching out for the cake pan.)*

Little Red Hen: *(With one hand she holds the pan over her head, out of their reach. She shakes a finger of her other hand and looks at the others as she speaks.)* Not so fast! Who found the wheat? Who planted the wheat? Who harvested the wheat? Who took the wheat to the miller to be ground into flour? Who made the flour into a cake? *(One by one, Duck, Cat, and Pig hang their heads in shame.)* It was I—Little Red Hen. I did it all by myself! So now my chicks and I will eat this cake all by ourselves! *(Duck, Cat, and Pig skulk off the stage with their heads hanging.)*

Narrator: And they did. *(Little Red Hen and chicks gather around the cake and begin eating it with much gusto.)*

The End

The Three Billy Goats Gruff

Cast

Narrator   _____   (nice clothes)

Troll   _____   (costume: page 32)

Big Billy Goat Gruff   _____   (costume: pages 32–37)

Bigger Billy Goat Gruff   _____   (costume: pages 32–37)

Biggest Billy Goat Gruff   _____   (costume: pages 32–37)

Props: long strip of blue fabric for stream, blue cushion for troll to land on, wooden bridge, green indoor/outdoor carpeting for grassy meadow

Setting: two fields with a river or stream separating them

Act 1

(Three billy goats are all grazing on the right-hand side of the river.)

Narrator: Once upon a time, there lived a family of three billy goat brothers whose last name was Gruff. The brothers liked nothing better than to eat as much grass as they could find.

Big Billy Goat: YUMMY! I love eating grass! I could eat grass all day and night!

Bigger Billy Goat: If you could find it.

Biggest Billy Goat: Hey, have you noticed that there isn't much grass left in this field? We've practically picked it clean.

Big Billy Goat and Bigger Billy Goat: *(together)* That's for sure!

The Three Billy Goats Gruff *(cont.)*

Biggest Billy Goat: I think we'd better find a new place to graze. I'll go look around. *(Walks around, staying on the right-hand side of the stage, and returns, shaking his head.)*

Bigger Billy Goat: What did you find?

Biggest Billy Goat: Nothing much. If only we could get to the other side of the river! There are no other goats over there. We could eat until our tummies were full! *(All three look longingly across the river.)*

Bigger Billy Goat: Let's try to swim across!

Big Billy Goat: But we don't know how to swim. *(Bigger Billy Goat jumps into the river and flails about as if drowning. The two others pull him out.)*

Big Billy Goat: You could have drowned!

Biggest Billy Goat: We'll just have to stay on this side of the river and make do with what grass is left. *(All three billy goats shake their heads sadly as they exit the stage.)*

Narrator: Actually, the three billy goats had eaten almost every single blade of grass. They would not make it through the summer on what little was left.

Setting: two fields separated by a river with a bridge connecting them and a troll hiding under the bridge

Narrator: Nearby, there was an evil troll who lived under the only bridge across the river. He would jump out and gobble up animals as they crossed the bridge. *(Troll comes out from under the bridge and speaks to the audience.)*

Troll: *(rubbing his hands and licking his lips)* I haven't had a tasty goat in ages. I hope one comes across this bridge soon! *(Troll goes back under the bridge.)*

The Three Billy Goats Gruff *(cont.)*

Act 2
(cont.)

Narrator: He didn't have long to wait, for the three Billy Goats Gruff were about to discover the bridge which led to the fields full of grass on the other side of the river. *(The three Billy Goats Gruff enter from the right and stop, startled at the sight of the bridge.)*

Big Billy Goat: Hey, look at that! I never knew there was a bridge across the river!

Bigger Billy Goat: I didn't either. Maybe the bridge is really a trap that the wolf has made just to catch us for dinner.

Biggest Billy Goat: *(nodding in agreement)* You may be right. It does seem too good to be true. Let's stay here for a day or two and watch the bridge carefully. Then we can see if it's safe to cross. *(All three billy goats exit the stage to the right. Then Big Billy Goat creeps back on stage from the right, looking back over his shoulder to be sure his brothers don't see him.)*

Big Billy Goat: *(to audience)* I'm not going to wait to get to that fabulous field of grass! I'm going over there right now! *(Big Billy Goat runs to the bridge. Troll jumps out and blocks his path halfway across the bridge.)*

Troll: Who's crossing my bridge? Why, it's a delicious goat! Just what I've been waiting for! Now I am going to eat you up! *(Troll grabs for Big Billy Goat, who steps back out of reach.)*

Big Billy Goat: Oh, you don't want to eat me. Just look at how thin and little I am. I would hardly make a meal for you.

Troll: A skinny little goat is better than no goat at all! You'd be a good snack! *(Troll again reaches for Big Billy Goat, who again steps back out of reach.)*

Big Billy Goat: Hold on! I tell you what. I'm the baby of the family. My bigger brother is coming after me, and he is MUCH fatter than I am. You wouldn't want to be so full from eating me that you couldn't eat the bigger goat, would you?

The Three Billy Goats Gruff *(cont.)*

Act 2
(cont.)

Troll: Oh, all right. But if your brother doesn't come, I'll find you and eat you!

Big Billy Goat: You can trust me. If he doesn't come, or if he isn't bigger as I've promised, then you can eat me.

(Troll steps aside and lets Big Billy Goat go across; then Troll hides under the bridge. Big Billy Goat begins to graze on the grass. Bigger Billy Goat enters from the right.)

Narrator: After a little while, Bigger Billy Goat came looking for his kid brother. *(Bigger Billy Goat comes to the bridge. Troll jumps out and blocks his path halfway across the bridge.)*

Troll: Who's crossing my bridge? Why, it's a delicious goat! Just what I've been waiting for! Now I am going to eat you up! *(Troll reaches for Bigger Billy Goat, who steps back out of reach.)*

Bigger Billy Goat: Oh, you don't want to eat me. Just look at how thin and bony I am. I would hardly make a meal for you.

Troll: A skinny goat is better than no goat at all! You'll be my meal! *(Troll again reaches out for Big Billy Goat, who again steps back out of reach.)*

Bigger Billy Goat: Hold on! I tell you what. I'm the middle goat of the family. My bigger brother is coming after me, and he is MUCH fatter and tastier than I am. You wouldn't want to be so full from eating me that you couldn't eat the bigger goat, would you?

Troll: Oh, all right. But if your brother doesn't come, I'll find you and eat you!

Bigger Billy Goat: You can trust me. If he doesn't come, or if he isn't bigger as I promised, then you can eat me.

(Troll steps aside and lets Bigger Billy Goat go across; then he hides under the bridge. Bigger Billy Goat joins Big Billy Goat in grazing on the grass. Biggest Billy Goat enters from the right.)

The Three Billy Goats Gruff *(cont.)*

Act 2
(cont.)

Narrator: Soon, Biggest Billy Goat came looking for his kid brothers. *(Biggest Billy Goat comes to the bridge. Troll jumps out and blocks his path across the bridge.)*

Troll: Who's crossing my bridge? Why, it's a delicious goat! Just what I've been waiting for! Now I am going to eat you up! *(Troll reaches for Biggest Billy Goat, who steps back out of reach.)*

Biggest Billy Goat: Oh, you don't want to eat me. Just look at how thin and scrawny I am. I would hardly make a meal for you.

Troll: Listen, your kid brothers came through here and promised me that I could eat you. You ARE the biggest of the goats, and I have worked up quite an appetite. So YOU are going to be MY DINNER. *(Troll again reaches for Biggest Billy Goat, who steps back, lowers his head, and butts Troll right over the edge of the bridge. Troll is pulled off the stage by means of a long strip of blue fabric, which is pulled to create the effect of a river current.)*

Biggest Billy Goat: *(Shouts over the edge of the bridge at Troll.)* You foolish troll! Not only am I the biggest of the Billy Goats Gruff, but I'm also the strongest and have the biggest horns! *(Biggest Billy Goat crosses the bridge and joins his brothers grazing on the grass.)*

Narrator: The evil troll was swept away by the current and never seen again. The Three Billy Goats Gruff stayed in the meadow and ate so much grass that they were never hungry again.

The End

The True Story of the Three Billy Goats Gruff as Told by A. Troll

Cast

Narrator	_____	(nice clothes)
Troll	_____	(costume: page 32)
Big Billy Goat Gruff	_____	(costume: pages 32–37)
Bigger Billy Goat Gruff	_____	(costume: pages 32–37)
Biggest Billy Goat Gruff	_____	(costume: pages 32–37)

Props: long strip of blue fabric for the stream, blue cushion for the troll to land on, wooden bridge, green indoor/outdoor carpeting for the grassy meadow, hammer

Setting: two fields with a river separating them

Act 1

(Three billy goats are all grazing on the right-hand side of the river.)

Narrator: Once upon a time, there lived a family of three billy goats whose last name was Gruff. The brothers liked nothing better than to fill their tummies with as much grass as they could find.

Big Billy Goat: YUMMY! I love eating grass! I could eat grass all day and all night!

Bigger Billy Goat: If you could find it!

Biggest Billy Goat: Hey, have you noticed that there isn't much grass left in this field? We've almost picked it clean.

Big Billy Goat and Bigger Billy Goat *(together)* Yes!

The True Story of the Three Billy Goats Gruff *(cont.)*

Biggest Billy Goat: Then we'd better find a new place to graze. I'll go look around. *(He walks around, staying on the right hand side of the stage, and returns to the others, shaking his head.)*

Bigger Billy Goat: What did you find?

Biggest Billy Goat: Nothing much. If only we could get to the other side of the river! There are no other goats over there. We could eat until our tummies were full! *(All three look longingly across the river.)*

Bigger Billy Goat: Let's try to swim across!

Big Billy Goat: But we don't know how to swim. *(Bigger Billy Goat jumps into the river and flails about as if drowning. The two others pull him out.)*

Big Billy Goat: You could have drowned!

Biggest Billy Goat: We'll just have to stay on this side of the river and make do with what grass is left. *(All three billy goats shake their heads sadly.)*

Narrator: Actually, the three billy goats had eaten almost every single blade of grass. They would not make it through the summer on what little was left.

Setting: two fields separated by a river with a bridge connecting them
(Troll is under the bridge, banging with a hammer as if building the bridge.)

Narrator: Nearby, there lived a handsome, hardworking troll. But the troll didn't have a job, and he needed money to buy food. So he decided to build a bridge across the river. That way he could earn money by charging those who wanted to cross the bridge.

The True Story of the Three Billy Goats Gruff *(cont.)*

Act 2
(cont.)

Troll: There, I think it's finished. *(He stands back to admire his work on the bridge.)* I can't wait for my first customer.

Narrator: He didn't have long to wait, for the three Billy Goats Gruff were about to discover this way to reach the fields of grass. *(The three billy goats enter from the right and stop, startled at the sight of the bridge.)*

Big Billy Goat: Hey, check it out! It looks like someone has built a bridge across the river.

Bigger Billy Goat: It does look like that! But what if it's a trap that the wolf has put up to catch us for dinner!

Biggest Billy Goat: *(nodding in agreement)* You may be right. It does seem too good to be true. Let's stay here for a day or two and watch the bridge carefully. Then we can see if it's a trap. *(All three billy goats exit the stage to the right; then Big Billy Goat sneaks back on stage and speaks to the audience.)*

Big Billy Goat: I'm not going to wait to get to that field of grass on the other side of the river! I'm going over there right now! *(Big Billy Goat runs toward the bridge. Troll steps out and blocks his path at the entrance to the bridge.)*

Troll: Good morning! Welcome to my toll bridge. In order to cross, you need to pay me fifty cents.

Big Billy Goat: I don't have fifty cents, and if I don't get to the grass on the other side of the river, I shall starve.

Troll: I'm sorry, but I built this bridge so I could make money. I can't let you cross if you don't pay me. I need to make a living just as much as you need that grass.

Big Billy Goat: I tell you what. I'm the baby of the family. My bigger brother is coming after me, and he will pay you for me as well as for himself. I promise you.

The True Story of Three Billy Goats Gruff *(cont.)*

Act 2
(cont.)

Troll: Oh, all right. But if your brother doesn't pay, I'll have no money to buy food. So I'll have to eat you.

Big Billy Goat: You can trust me. You'll get your money, or you can eat me. *(Troll steps aside and lets Big Billy Goat go across. Then Troll goes and sits under the bridge. Big Billy Goat begins to graze on the grass.)*

Narrator: In a little while, Bigger Billy Goat came looking for his kid brother. *(Troll steps out and blocks his path at the entrance to the bridge.)*

Troll: Good morning! Welcome to my toll bridge. In order to cross, you need to pay me fifty cents for you and fifty cents for your younger brother. He promised me you'd pay his toll as well as your own. That's $1.00 altogether.

Bigger Billy Goat: I don't have $1.00 or even fifty cents, and if I don't get to the grass on the other side of the river, I shall starve!

Troll: I'm sorry, but I built this bridge so I could make money. I can't let you cross if you don't pay me. I need to make a living just as much as you need that grass.

Bigger Billy Goat: I'll tell you what. I'm the middle goat of the family. My bigger brother is coming after me, and he will pay you for all of us. I promise you.

Troll: Oh, all right. But if your brother doesn't pay, I'll have no money to buy food. So I'll have to eat you.

Bigger Billy Goat: You can trust me. You'll get your money or you can eat me. *(Troll steps aside and lets Bigger Billy Goat go across. Troll then goes and sits under the bridge. Bigger Billy Goat joins his brother in grazing on the grass.)*

Narrator: Soon Biggest Billy Goat came looking for his kid brothers. *(Troll steps out and blocks his path at the entrance to the bridge.)*

The True Story of the Three Billy Goats Gruff *(cont.)*

Act 2
(cont.)

Troll: Good morning! Welcome to my toll bridge. In order to cross, you need to pay me fifty cents for each of your younger brothers. They promised me you'd pay their tolls as well as your own. That's $1.50 altogether.

Biggest Billy Goat: I don't have $1.50 or even fifty cents, and if I don't get to the grass on the other side of the river, I shall starve!

Troll: I'm sorry, but I built this bridge so I could make money. I can't let you cross if you don't pay me. I need to make a living just as much as you need that grass.

Biggest Billy Goat: All right, I'll pay you what you deserve. Please step closer to me. *(Troll gets much closer to Biggest Billy Goat, and Biggest Billy Goat butts him with his head so hard that the troll plunges into the river. Then Biggest Billy Goat crosses the bridge and joins his brothers grazing on the grass.)*

Troll: *(Emerging from the river, he faces the audience to speak.)* Well, they won't pay me, and I need to eat. I told them what I'd do if they didn't pay. I guess I'll just have to go eat one of them. *(He goes to the field and tries to grab Bigger Billy Goat. The other two billy goats butt him back into the river.)*

Troll: *(Emerging from the river, he faces the audience to speak.)* This toll bridge is just not working out. I think I'll go build a mall. Maybe I'll have better luck with that. *(He leaves the stage, shoulders slumped, and shaking his head sadly.)*

Narrator: Now you finally know the TRUE story of the Three Billy Goats Gruff. I know it's the truth because I heard it from the troll himself!

The End

Goldilocks and the Three Bears

Cast

Narrator _____ (nice clothes)

Goldilocks _____ (costume: nice clothes)

Mama Bear _____ (costume: pages 61–63)

Papa Bear _____ (costume: pages 61–63)

Baby Bear _____ (costume: pages 61–63)

Skunks _____ (costume: pages 53–57)

Raccoons _____ (costume: page 48)

Birds _____ (costume: pages 39–45)

Honeybees _____ (costume: page 64–65)

Flowers _____ (costume: pages 68–73)

Props: table settings for three, table, three chairs of differing sizes *(a rocker for the smallest)*, three beds of differing sizes (You can make the beds by placing plywood on two cardboard boxes of the same height.), pillows, pancakes, a cardboard house front with doors and windows cut into it, bucket or bowl of berries

Setting: For this play, the forest scene is painted onto large sheets of butcher paper and tacked, taped, or tied onto the background wall or curtain of your stage.

Goldilocks and the Three Bears *(cont.)*

Scene 1

Narrator *(older student)*: Hi, everyone! Have I got a story to tell you today!

Down the road a bit from my grandma's, near the woods, lives a little girl. Her name is Mary—no, it's Jane . . . or was it Matilda? Oh well, I'll just call her Goldilocks because her soft, yellow curls look like shiny, spun gold. Goldilocks may look like an angel, but she often doesn't act like one. She has a way of not minding her mother, which often gets her into a lot of trouble—like what happened yesterday. This is the way the story goes. . . .

(a clearing in the woods near the bears' home)

Enter forest animals: *(skunks, rabbits, raccoons, birds, honeybees buzzing near flowers—all singing to the tune of "Good Morning to You")*

> Good morning to you,
>
> This bright shiny day!
>
> I'm happy to see you—
>
> Come, let's work and play!

(Animals greet one another, shaking hands, hugging, saying "Hi, how are you?" etc.)

Enter Baby Bear: Good morning! Mom's making my very favorite breakfast. I bet you can't guess what it is!

Forest Animals: *(in unison)* Pancakes!

Baby Bear: Yum, yum! I love pancakes!

Enter Mama Bear: *(Baby Bear sees Mama Bear and speaks.)*

Baby Bear: It's time to eat! Here I come!

Mama Bear: Sorry, Son, but the pancakes are much too hot to eat. Let's go for a walk in the forest to see the new baby ducklings at the lake. We can also pick some fresh berries to eat with our pancakes.

Baby Bear: *(with a pout)* Okay, but I'm awfully hungry.

Goldilocks and the Three Bears *(cont.)*

Scene 1
(cont.)

Mama Bear: Come on, Papa Bear, let's go. Our friends are waiting to go with us.

Papa Bear: *(in a great big voice)* What are we waiting for? Let's go! *(All exit.)*

Enter Goldilocks: *(singing to "Skip to My Lou")*

Skip, skip, skip into the woods,

Chase butterflies and ladybugs too,

Listen to the honeybees buzzing in their hive,

I'm skipping in the woods this morning.

Scene 2

(Home of the Three Bears)

Goldilocks *(cont.):* Oh, what a cute house! I wonder who lives here? Hmmm. I'll just peek into this window to see. *(She peeks into window.)* The curtain's in the way, and I can't see a thing! I'll try the keyhole. *(Peeks through the keyhole, and the door swings open.)* Oops, the door is open. Hello! Is anyone at home? Looks like no one's at home. Perhaps some dwarfs live here like in Snow White. What is that delicious smell? I'm hungry! *(Goldilocks walks to the table and stops at Baby Bear's plate. She picks up a fork and then puts it down.)* This is too little. I'm very hungry! *(She walks to Mama Bear's plate, picks up a fork, and tastes a bite.)*

This is too dry. Yuk! *(She turns to Papa Bear's plate and picks up his fork.)*

Wow, this pancake is big! Hope it tastes good. *(She tastes.)*

Yummy, this is good! *(She eats up all his pancakes. After eating, Goldilocks walks into the living room.)*

Hmmm, chairs. A great big one! Must be for a papa. *(She climbs into the chair.)*

This is not comfortable—it's too hard! I'll try that cute little rocker. *(She squeezes in.)*

Too tight! Oh, well. I'll try the one that looks like a mama's chair. It has flowers on the pillows like my mom's. *(Goldilocks climbs in and fluffs the pillow to sit on. As she fluffs it, she tears it, and some of the stuffing falls out.)*

Oops! I hope this mama can fix this.

Goldilocks and the Three Bears *(cont.)*

Scene 2
(cont.)

Goldilocks: *(Goldilocks walks into the bedroom and lies down on Papa Bear's bed, tossing and turning a bit.)*

This bed is too hard! *(She walks to Mama Bear's bed and sees the flowery pillows there, too.)*

I'd better not sleep on her bed. I've already ruined one of her pillows. *(She walks to Baby Bear's bed, decorated in a child's print.)*

This is a little bit too cutesy for me, but it is more my size, and I'm very tired. I think I'll take a short nap and then start for home before Mom starts looking for me. *(Goldilocks falls asleep.)*

Scene 3

(Kitchen: Enter Three Bears)

Mama Bear: Baby Bear, put the berries on the kitchen table, please.

Baby Bear: *(walks to the table and cries out . . .)* What a mess! Looks like somebody's been tasting our pancakes!

Papa Bear: *(in a deep voice)* Goodness gracious! Someone ate up all my pancakes! Let's see if the pancake snatcher is still here. Get behind me and keep quiet. *(Bears all tiptoe to the living room.)*

Mama Bear: Goodness gracious! Look at this! My favorite pillow is ruined! *(Sobs.)* Let's see if the pillow ripper is still here. Get behind me and keep quiet. *(Bears all tiptoe to the bedroom.)*

Baby Bear: Goodness gracious! The pancake snitcher-pillow ripper is in my bed! *(Bears all rush to the bed, and Goldilocks jumps up.)*

Goldilocks: Goodness gracious! Three bears! *(Goldilocks screams and runs out.)*

Mama Bear: She was not a very polite little girl.

Baby Bear: Too bad. We could have been friends. I would have shared my berries and pancakes with her.

Mama Bear: This was enough excitement for one day. Let's go to the kitchen and I'll make you some more pancakes.

Papa Bear: Goodness gracious! I sure am hungry!

The End

It's Just a Dollar

Teacher's Note: You may want to divide the banker's role into two parts by casting a Mr. and Ms. Banker.

Cast

Child 1	_____	(regular clothing)
Child 2	_____	(regular clothing)
Child 3	_____	(regular clothing)
Child 4	_____	(regular clothing)
Ms. Banker	_____	(green sun visor, nice clothes)
Pig E. Bank	_____	(costume: pages 23–28)

Props: large cardboard cutouts made to look like a nickel, a dime, a quarter, and a dollar bill, mini-baseball cap with label—"Pig E. Bank"

Setting: sidewalk in a small town, modern times

(As the curtain opens, children 1–4 are standing in the center of the stage. Each has the appropriate coin or dollar bill.)

Child 1: *(comes forward and holds up coin)* I found a nickel as I walked along the street. I'll use it to buy something good to eat.

Child 2: *(comes forward and holds up coin)* I've got a quarter, and I don't know what to buy—a candy bar, a pack of gum, or some tasty French fries.

Child 3: *(comes forward and holds up coin)* I've got a dime my father gave to me. Now I can go on a spending spree!

Child 4: *(comes forward and holds up a dollar bill)* I earned a dollar for raking my neighbor's lawn. I'll spend it on a creepy crawler or a beanbag fawn.

(Ms. Banker enters from the right and comes up to the children.)

It's Just a Dollar *(cont.)*

Ms. Banker: Good morning, children. I couldn't help but overhear, and it seems to me that you're determined to make your money disappear. But why spend your money? Just think what it could do—for if you put it in the bank, it would grow and grow for you!

Child 4: It's just a dollar!

Child 3: Mine's just worth ten cents!

Child 2: I've only got a quarter!

Child 1: It might as well be spent. *(pause)* And anyway, my nickel's got a dent.

Child 2: You can't stop us from spending our money any way we please!

Child 3: Why do you care if we go on spending sprees?

Ms. Banker: Once you've spent your money, you won't have it any more. You will have to give it to the person at the store. But money put into a bank makes more money, almost as fast as bees make honey.

There's this special thing called interest. It makes money in a bank account grow. So the longer your money's in a bank, the more money you'll have to show.

Child 4: She's right! After all, two nickels make a dime. Four quarters make a dollar. And given lots of time, our coins and dollars can become a gold mine!

Ms. Banker: Now here comes someone I'd like you to meet. When it comes to saving money, he just can't be beat. He's round and plump and jolly, indeed. And he wants very much to see you succeed.
(Pig E. Bank enters from right and goes up to the children.)

Pig E. Bank: Please let me introduce myself. I am Pig E. Bank, and if you want to save your money, just fill up my tank.

I'm pleased with dimes and nickels, and I like quarters too. Any money that you get, I'd like to save for you.

Child 2: Filling you with money sounds like something I'd like to do. But where do we get the money to put inside of you?

It's Just a Dollar *(cont.)*

Pig E. Bank: Do you get money for birthday presents? *(All four children nod.)* Then put it in me along with your weekly allowance. *(Pig E. Bank leans forward as if sharing a secret but still speaks loudly and clearly.)*

I'll tell you a secret few people know—now listen closely to this info: Save your pennies and nickels and especially dimes, for a fortune is made one nickel at a time. *(last part spoken slowly and with emphasis)*

So when I'm full of money, how rich you each will be! You'll be very pleased with what you've got. You have my personal guarantee!

Ms. Banker: And once you've filled up Pig E. Bank, please bring him to me at the SAVE RIGHT BANK. I'll open an account for you. Then every time that you come back, you'll find your money grew!

Child 1: I think I'll save my nickel.

Child 2: I'll save my quarter, too. *(looks at Child 3)* What about you?

Child 3: I guess I'll save my dime 'cause it really sounds like fun to save every coin I get and count them when I'm done.

Child 4: I want to keep my hard-earned dollar. My birthday's coming soon, so I can ask for the creepy crawler.

Pig E. Bank: You've made my day, for now I know you'll feed me when you can. *(points with thumb to chest)* This Pig E. Bank likes money instead of toast with jam.

Ms. Banker: *(shakes each child's hand as she speaks)* I'm proud of every one of you. In fact, you've made my day, too. By learning to be a frequent saver, you've done yourselves a great big favor.

All: *(Cast faces audience and joins hands as they speak.)* So never say "It's just a dollar," for now you know it's true that even dimes and nickels can bring benefits to you. Any money can be the beginning of a bank account; you can start one with any amount.

Ms. Banker: *(releases hands and steps forward)* This is where our story ends. We hope you'll think before you spend.

The End

Talent Search

Cast

Narrator 1   _____ (nice clothes)

Narrator 2   _____ (nice clothes)

Narrator 3   _____ (nice clothes)

Boy   _____ (overalls)

Rabbit   _____ (costume: pages 59 and 60)

Beaver   _____ (costume: page 58)

Fox   _____ (costume: pages 50–52)

Hen   _____ (costume: pages 17–19)

Owl   _____ (costume: pages 44–45)

Props: log, spade, big rock, tree, toy axe, henhouse

Setting: rural area

Act 1

Narrator 1: Once there was a little boy whose brother and sister were very talented. His sister could play the flute, and his brother could draw. The little boy did not have any talent, and he felt left out. So one day he went in search of his own talent.

(Little boy enters, walking slowly from right, and Rabbit enters from the left, both stopping when they meet each other in center stage.)

Rabbit: Hello, Little Boy.

Boy: Hi, Rabbit. I am searching for talent all my own. Do you know where I can find it?

Talent Search *(cont.)*

Rabbit: Why, of course I do! Go over to that rock beside that old log. *(Rabbit points.)* Dig between the rock and the log, and you will find your talent.

Boy: Oh, thank you, Rabbit!

(Little Boy runs offstage and immediately returns carrying a spade. He goes over to the rock and log and pantomimes digging a deep hole. Rabbit stands near him, pantomiming as if urging him on.)

Narrator 1: The little boy dug for an hour without stopping. By then the hole was very deep.

Boy: Rabbit, I have dug without stopping at all. But I do not see any talent. Are you sure this is the right place to dig?

Rabbit: Yes, this is the place to dig.

(Little Boy continues to pantomime digging. He stops and wipes his brow with the back of his hand. Looking exhausted, he turns to face the rabbit.)

Boy: There is no talent here, Rabbit!

Rabbit: You're right. But there is a lovely new home for me. Thank you, Little Boy.

(Rabbit bustles into the hole the boy has dug. Little Boy gives a shocked and exasperated look to the audience and then shrugs and leaves the stage.)

Narrator 2: The little boy was upset because the rabbit had tricked him. But he continued his search for talent.

(Little Boy enters from the right, and Beaver enters from the left, both stopping when they meet in center stage.)

Beaver: Hello, Little Boy.

Boy: Hi, Beaver. I am searching for talent all my own. Do you know where I can find it?

Talent Search *(cont.)*

Act 2
(cont.)

Beaver: I certainly do! *(points)* If you cut that tree down, you will be able to get your talent.

Boy: Oh, thank you, Beaver!

(Little Boy runs offstage and immediately returns carrying an axe. He goes over to the tree that the beaver pointed out and pantomimes chopping it down. Beaver stands by and pantomimes encouraging him to continue.)

Narrator 2: The little boy chopped for an hour without stopping. By then the tree was ready to fall. *(Little Boy stops to rest and wipes his brow with the back of his hand.)*

Boy: Beaver, I haven't seen any talent yet. Are you sure this is the right tree?

Beaver: Yes, this is the tree. Knock it down!

(Little Boy gives the tree a big push. It topples to the ground. Then he stops and wipes his brow with the back of his hand. Looking exhausted, he turns to face the beaver.)

Boy: There is no talent here, Beaver!

Beaver: You're right. But there is a wonderful log to add to my den. Thank you, Little Boy.

(Beaver picks up the log and drags it offstage to the left. Boy gives a shocked and exasperated look to the audience and then shrugs and leaves the stage.)

Act 3

Narrator 3: The little boy was discouraged because the beaver had fooled him. But he continued his search for talent.

(Little Boy enters from the right, and Fox enters from the left, both stopping when they meet at center stage.)

Talent Search *(cont.)*

Act 3
(cont.)

Fox: Hello, Little Boy.

Boy: Hi, Fox. I am searching for talent. Do you know where I can find it?

Fox: Sure I do! The talent is hidden inside your henhouse. Take me there, and I will show you.

Boy: Thank you, Fox! Let's run!
(Little Boy and Fox run offstage to the right. Curtain closes long enough to allow for setup of the henhouse and tree. Then the curtain reopens, and the boy and the fox approach the henhouse. They appear breathless from running. The little boy wipes his brow with the back of his hand.)

Fox: Open the door very quietly. You don't want to disturb the talent. *(Fox glances around to be sure they are alone.)* Hurry and open the door!

(Little Boy opens the henhouse door. The hen jumps out through the door and is instantly snatched by Fox. Fox grabs the loudly clucking hen by the wrist and runs with her off the stage to the left. Meanwhile, the little boy has his head stuck inside, looking for his talent. Finally, he withdraws his head and speaks.)

Boy: There is no talent in here, Fox!

Fox: You're right. But there is a delicious dinner for me. Thank you, Little Boy!

Narrator 3: When the little boy realized that the wicked fox had stolen a hen, he began to cry.
(Boy stumbles over to the tree, sits down, and covers his face with his hands, sobbing. Owl comes from behind the tree.)

Owl: Who-o-o-o is crying under my tree?

Boy: *(tearful voice)* It's me, Owl. I can't help crying. I've had an awful day!

Owl: Perhaps I can help you. Tell me what's wrong.

Talent Search *(cont.)*

Act 3
(cont.)

Boy: My sister can play the flute, and my brother can draw anything. But I have no talent, so I went searching for talent. I met a rabbit who told me to dig a deep hole. I dug for an hour without stopping, but I didn't find any talent. Then I met a beaver who told me to cut down a tree. I chopped the tree down, but I didn't find any talent. Then I met a fox who told me to look in my henhouse, but there was no talent there. And, worst of all, he ate one of our hens! Owl, do you know where I can find talent?

Owl: You already have what is needed for talent.

Boy: What do you mean?

Owl: Talent takes determination and hard work, for a talent must be practiced. You have shown determination and worked very hard today in your search for talent. But talent cannot be found. It is a gift. If you could choose any talent, what would it be?

Boy: I have always wanted to sing.

Owl: Then I will give you a beautiful singing voice. Each time you sing, your voice will grow stronger. But if you don't keep using your talent, you will lose it.

Boy: *(grabs his throat and sings)* Do-re-me-fa-so-la-ti-do! *(speaks)* Oh, thank you, Owl! *(sings enthusiastically to the tune of "Twinkle, Twinkle, Little Star")*

Thank you, Owl, for this gracious gift!

When people sing and voices lift,

I will be able to sing along

With a voice both clear and strong.

Thank you, Owl; thank you so!

And now it's time for me to go.

(Boy and Owl link arm and wing and walk off the stage together to the right.)

The End

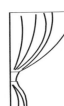

Why Butterflies Are So Colorful

Teacher's Note: Butterflies have warning coloration. During the larval stage they eat plants with bitter or poisonous juices. These are stored in their exoskeletons, making them taste awful. Butterflies' bright colors testify to this, and as a result, they are avoided by predators. Thus, once they survive their caterpillar and cocoon stages, butterflies are almost never eaten.

Cast

(This cast may be expanded to include all class members by adding additional birds, more plain butterflies, and extra flowers.)

Narrator 1 _____ (regular clothes)

Narrator 2 _____ (regular clothes)

Narrator 3 _____ (regular clothes)

Skunk _____ (costume: pages 53–57)

Beautiful Butterfly _____ (costume: pages 66 and 67)

Plain Butterfly 1 _____ (costume: pages 66 and 67)

Plain Butterfly 2 _____ (costume: pages 66 and 67)

Plain Butterfly 3 _____ (costume: pages 66 and 67)

Why Butterflies Are So Colorful *(cont.)*

Cast *(cont.)*

Bird _____ (costume: pages 39–43)

Birds in flock—First _____ (costumes: pages 39–43)

Second _____

Third _____

Fourth _____

Fifth _____

Owl _____ (costume: pages 44 and 45)

Pink Flower _____ (costume: pages 68–73)

Yellow Flower _____ (costume: pages 68–73)

Orange Flower _____ (costume: pages 68–73)

Props: water-filled squirt gun, two trees or bunches of branches, three cans of powder for "magic dust"

Setting: meadow in summer

Act 1

Narrator 1: Long ago, butterflies were a plain, dull, light brown color. There was one butterfly, though, that was born very colorful. *(Beautiful Butterfly comes on stage from the right and begins to pantomime flying about the meadow.)* The other butterflies thought that he was odd and made him feel unwelcome. So the beautiful butterfly learned to avoid the other butterflies. He became good friends with a skunk. *(Skunk enters from the left, and the two pantomime talking and laughing together.)* The skunk knew just how the beautiful butterfly felt because she too was often disliked and avoided by other animals.

Why Butterflies Are So Colorful *(cont.)*

Act 1
(cont.)

Skunk: Beautiful Butterfly, how happy I am that we are friends! I can always count on you to be happy to see me. You would never turn and run away like the other meadow animals do when they see me coming. My life would be very lonely without you!

Beautiful Butterfly: I'm glad that you're my friend, too. None of the other butterflies like me just because I am the wrong colors. But I know I can talk to you about anything and you'll understand. You always know how to make me laugh.

Narrator 1: While they were talking, they did not notice a big bird swooping down for the Beautiful Butterfly. *(Bird enters from left and flaps gracefully yet silently across the stage, suddenly grabbing the Beautiful Butterfly.)* Before they knew what was happening, the Beautiful Butterfly was in the bird's beak about to be his lunch. The skunk reacted instantly. He lifted his tail and aimed straight for the bird's head. *(Skunk turns to face the audience, bends over, and shoots water gun from under his tail, hitting Bird in the face.)*

Bird: *(sputtering and dropping hold on Beautiful Butterfly)* Oh, no! Ugh! I can't stand it! Get it away from me! *(Bird pushes Beautiful Butterfly away and rushes across the stage, exiting left.)*

Beautiful Butterfly: Oh, Skunk, you saved me! How can I ever thank you?

Skunk: By being my best friend forever.

Act 2

Setting: tree branches full of birds in front right corner and another set in the rear left corner

Bird: *(rushing in from left)* I've just had the most awful experience!

First Bird in Flock: It can't be any worse than how you smell!

Second Bird in Flock: Get out of this tree! I can't stand the smell! *(Covers beak with hands.)*

Why Butterflies Are So Colorful *(cont.)*

Third Bird in Flock: Look out! I'm about to toss my worms! *(makes gagging sounds and holds throat)*

Fourth Bird in Flock: Stay away from me! I think I'm going to faint! *(wobbles on branch)*

Fifth Bird in Flock: Why don't you fly over to that tree over there *(points across stage to far corner)* and tell us what in the world happened to you?

Bird: *(flies to far corner before speaking)* I saw the strangest butterfly. It was brightly colored. I'd never seen one like it before. Of course, butterflies are my favorite food, so I wanted to eat it. But when I picked it up, this is what happened to me!

I know I smell horrible. But the taste in my mouth is absolutely unbearable! I'll never eat a colorful butterfly again as long as I live, and you'd better not try it, either! *(holds stomach and groans)* I feel like tossing my worms!

Setting: meadow in summer, group of three plain butterflies gathered at center stage

Narrator 2: The birds listened to their friend and decided never to eat a colorful butterfly. They also warned every bird they met. Meanwhile, the dull brown butterflies noticed that the birds never bothered the colorful butterfly, even when he was out in plain sight.

Plain Butterfly 1: Do you have any idea why the birds have a big appetite for us but totally ignore that weird misfit butterfly?

Plain Butterfly 2: No, but I wish I knew what his secret is. I'm tired of always being afraid and constantly watching out for these lousy birds!
(Beautiful Butterfly enters stage from right, flapping wings gracefully, humming happily.)

Plain Butterfly 3: Well, there he is now! Let's ask him.

Why Butterflies Are So Colorful *(cont.)*

Act 3
(cont.)

Plain Butterfly 1: I certainly don't intend to talk to the likes of him!

Plain Butterfly 2: Me neither!

Plain Butterfly 3: Suit yourselves. But I'm not too proud to ask his secret if it can save my life! *(flies over to Beautiful Butterfly)* Hello! I was wondering. Why don't the birds ever try to eat you? They're ALWAYS trying to eat us.

Beautiful Butterfly: I think it's because of my awful colors. They don't like them any better than the rest of you do. I guess I'm such a misfit that the birds won't even eat me.

Plain Butterfly 3: Better to be a misfit like you than to be a bird's supper! How do I get to be colorful like you?

Beautiful Butterfly: YOU want to be like ME?

Plain Butterfly 3: Yes, I do. Now please tell me. How do I get to be colorful like you?

Beautiful Butterfly: I really don't know. I was born this way. *(pauses, then brightens)* But my friend Skunk always goes to see Owl whenever she has an important question. Maybe Owl can tell you how to look like me.

Plain Butterfly 3: Isn't an owl a BIRD? I'm not crazy enough to visit a bird for any reason! What are you trying to do—get me killed?

Beautiful Butterfly: *(indignantly)* Of course not! Actually I've never been to see Owl myself. Whenever I have an important question, Skunk asks for me. Would you like me to ask Skunk to visit Owl with your question?

Plain Butterfly 3: Yes, please.

Why Butterflies Are So Colorful *(cont.)*

Act 4

Setting: Owl sleeping in tree branches, snoring loudly

Narrator 2: Beautiful Butterfly asked Skunk to visit Owl with Plain Butterfly's question. So Skunk set off to see Owl. *(Skunk enters from the right and creeps up to the snoring Owl.)*

Skunk: Oh, Owl, are you awake? *(Snoring continues, so Skunk asks again more loudly.)* Hey, Owl, are you awake? *(Snoring continues, so Skunk shouts.)* OWL, WAKE UP!

Owl: *(Startled awake, she speaks in an annoyed tone.)* Who-o-o-o-o is disturbing me while I'm trying to sleep?

Skunk: I'm sorry, Owl, but I need the answer to a most difficult question. I hope that you will tell me, for you are the wisest creature in the whole meadow.

Owl: What's the question?

Skunk: A plain butterfly wants to know how she can become colorful like my best friend.

Owl: It is a good thing you came to ask me, for I am the only creature who knows the answer. My great-great-uncle loved to mix potions and powders as his hobby. I have some of his magic dust. When sprinkled on a flower, it causes the flower to rub its color off on anything that touches it. And it doesn't hurt the flower at all.

Skunk: Will you give me some of this magic dust?

Owl: Yes, if you will help me. I would like to have some of your "perfume" in a tightly capped bottle. I think it could come in very handy the next time an eagle tries to grab my owlets.

Skunk: No problem. It's a deal.

Why Butterflies Are So Colorful *(cont.)*

Act 5

Setting: meadow in summer

Narrator 3: So Skunk got the magic dust for his friend Beautiful Butterfly. Beautiful Butterfly took it to the Plain Butterfly who had convinced several other butterflies that it was wise to be colorful. Plain Butterfly invited Beautiful Butterfly to come with them when they used the magic dust. *(The three plain butterflies and Beautiful Butterfly enter from the right and fly to center stage. The flowers enter from the left and stay toward the back of the stage, standing very still.)*

Plain Butterfly 1: *(grumbles to Plain Butterfly 3)* Why does he have to come along?

Plain Butterfly 3: Because he's the one who got the magic dust for us, you ungrateful bug!
(They both pantomime flying about the stage, flapping wings, going in an S pattern rather than a straight line to the flowers.)

Narrator 3: They flew to a place full of flowers. Each plain butterfly picked a flower on which to sprinkle the magic dust . Then the butterflies rubbed against the flowers. *(Butterflies each pick a different-colored flower and sprinkle magic dust on it and then rub their wings against it.)* Sure enough, their wings turned the color of the flower each had chosen. *(The butterflies pull off the plain brown paper coverings from their wings to reveal the colorful wings beneath. Then they pantomime flying about the stage, flapping their wings. They go in an S pattern toward home.)* On their way home, several birds approached them. *(Birds enter from the right and head straight for butterflies.)*

First and Second Birds in Flock: Oh, no! It's a whole group of those awful colored butterflies! *(They flap their wings frantically and rush offstage.)*

Why Butterflies Are So Colorful *(cont.)*

Act 5
(cont.)

Third and Fourth Birds in Flock: I'm getting out of here! *(flap wings frantically and rush offstage)*

Fifth Bird in Flock: This meadow isn't big enough for us and them. Let's find a new place to live! *(flaps wings frantically and rushes off stage)*

Used-to-Be-Plain Butterfly 3: It worked: we scared those terrible birds away. We won't have to live in fear anymore.

Used-to-Be-Plain Butterfly 2: You're right! Oh, I'm so happy we did this. Thank you, Beautiful Butterfly. You're a hero!

Used-to-Be-Plain Butterfly 1: *(grumbles)* I wouldn't go that far.

Used-to-Be-Plain Butterfly 3: *(to Beautiful Butterfly)* I'm ashamed of the way we treated you just because you were different. Please forgive us and come to live with us.

Beautiful Butterfly: I forgive you, but I don't want to live with you. I want to be with my best friend, Skunk. She's never cared what I looked like. She has always been my loyal friend, and I will stay with her as long as I live. *(Skunk comes onto the stage and links arms with Beautiful Butterfly.)*

The End

108

The Girl Who Would Be Queen

Cast

Narrator 1 _____ (regular clothes)

Narrator 2 _____ (regular clothes)

Old Woman _____ (old clothes)

Cow _____ (costume: pages 29–31)

Pig _____ (costume: pages 23–28)

Sheep _____ (costume: page 38)

Rachel _____ (nice clothes)

Laura _____ (nice clothes)

Katrina _____ (nice clothes)

Queen _____ (nice clothes; crown, page 74)

Prince Edward _____ (nice clothes; crown, page 74)

Prince Matthew _____ (nice clothes; crown, page 74)

Prince John _____ (nice clothes; crown, page 74)

Props: fireplace, table, two chairs, two soup bowls, two spoons, cooking pot, countertop with dishpan and drainboard, stove, bucket, water to fill bucket, hay, small pan filled with corn kernels, logs, bed

The Girl Who Would Be Queen *(cont.)*

Act 1

Setting: old hut in the forest with cow, pig, and sheep in front of fireplace and old woman sitting at a table

Narrator 1: *(reads before curtains open)* Once there lived a queen with magical powers who had triplet sons. When it came time for them to marry, the Queen could not choose which one should rule as king. She also feared that her sons might choose for brides beautiful girls who were foolish, selfish, or vain. So the Queen came up with a plan to solve both of her worries.
(curtain opens)

Cow: Mother, are you sure this plan will work?

Old Woman: Yes, my darling. No one will ever guess who we are or that this *(waves to indicate hut)* is really a castle.

Pig: But how will we ever find suitable wives this way?

Old Woman: I have placed a spell on the whole forest so that every maiden who enters it will lose her way and stop here, seeking shelter for the night.

Sheep: Once she's here, then what?

Old Woman: Don't worry. It will all become clear. *(Rachel enters stage and knocks on door of hut.)* The first maiden is here now. *(Old Woman goes to door and opens it.)*

Rachel: Hello. My name is Rachel. I lost my way in the forest, and it's grown too dark to go on. May I please stay here tonight?

Old Woman: You may stay if you will prepare my evening meal.

The Girl Who Would Be Queen *(cont.)*

Act 1
(cont.)

Rachel: Sure, *(in bragging tone)* that will be easy for me. I'm a good cook! *(Rachel enters and Old Woman shows her to the kitchen. Rachel immediately begins to pantomime cooking a meal. Old Woman goes back over and sits down at the table. Rachel finishes cooking.)* Here's your meal. *(Both eat the soup.)*

Old Woman: This soup is delicious! You are a good cook!

Rachel: Thank you. Now I'm tired. Please show me to my bed.

Old Woman: Certainly, Rachel. *(Old Woman opens a door facing back of stage, and Rachel enters.)* Sleep well.

Rachel: Good night. *(She closes door.)*

Cow: Is she the one?

Old Woman: No, she is not.

Sheep: But why not?

Old Woman: I will tell you why in the morning.

Narrator 1: The next morning, Rachel woke up and ate a meal made by the Old Woman. Then she went on her way.

Pig: Mother, why did you let her go? She was pretty, and you said yourself that she's a good cook!

Old Woman: It's not important for a queen to be a good cook. And beauty fades with time. Don't worry, dear sons, I will find each of you a suitable bride. *(Laura enters stage and knocks on door of hut.)* Here's another maiden already. *(Old Woman goes to door and opens it.)* Good evening. What can I do for you?

Laura: Hello. My name is Laura. I lost my way in the forest, and it's grown too dark to go on. May I please stay here tonight?

Old Woman: You may stay if you will prepare my evening meal.

The Girl Who Would Be Queen *(cont.)*

Act 1
(cont.)

Laura: Thank you very much! I'll make your evening meal. Just tell me what you would like to eat. *(Laura enters and Old Woman shows her to the kitchen. Laura immediately begins to pantomime cooking a meal. Old Woman goes back over and sits down at the table.)* Here's our meal. I hope you like it. *(Both eat the stew.)*

Old Woman: This stew is delicious! You are a good cook!

Laura: Thank you. *(She picks up bowls and pantomimes washing them in the sink. When she finishes, she turns to the Old Woman.)* I'm very tired. Please show me to my bed.

Old Woman: Certainly, Laura. *(Old Woman opens the door facing back of stage, and Laura enters.)* Sleep well.

Laura: Good night, and thanks again. *(She closes door.)*

Sheep: Is she the one?

Old Woman: No, she is not.

Cow: But why not?

Old Woman: I will tell you in the morning.

Narrator 1: The next morning Laura woke up and made a tasty meal for herself and the Old Woman. Then after washing the dishes, she went on her way.

Pig: Mother, why did you let her go? She was a good cook and very lovely. And she was so polite that she made your breakfast and did the dishes after BOTH meals!

Old Woman: She was lovely and polite, but there is something more that I seek. Don't worry, dear sons, I will find each of you a suitable bride. *(Katrina enters and knocks on the door of the hut.)* Here is another maiden. *(Old Woman goes to the door and opens it.)*

The Girl Who Would Be Queen *(cont.)*

Act 1
(cont.)

Old Woman: Good evening. What can I do for you?

Katrina: Hello. My name is Katrina. I lost my way in the forest, and it's grown too dark to go on. May I please stay here tonight?

Old Woman: You may stay if you will prepare my evening meal.

Katrina: Thank you so much! I'll gladly make your evening meal. I only hope that I can please you with my cooking. What would you like me to make? *(Katrina enters, and Old Woman shows her to the kitchen. Katrina immediately begins to pantomime cooking a meal. Old Woman goes back over and sits down at the table.)*

Katrina: *(coming to the table from kitchen area)* While the pot is simmering, may I get some food and water for the animals?

Old Woman: Yes. You will find hay for the cow and sheep and corn for the pig just outside the front door. Draw some water in this bucket *(hands her a bucket from under the table)* from our well. Thank you. *(Katrina leaves through front door and goes offstage, returning with a bucketful of water which she places before the animals. They gather around as if drinking. Then Katrina leaves again, goes offstage, and returns with an armload of hay and a small pan of corn. She places the food before the animals. While they eat, she stands and pets each one lovingly.)*

Katrina: *(clasping her cheeks in alarm)* Oh, dear! I forgot about dinner! Oh, I hope I haven't burned it! *(She rushes to the stove and then brings a bowl to Old Woman, seated at the table.)* Here's our meal. I'm terrible sorry that it's overdone. *(Both eat.)*

Old Woman: Don't worry. It's fine.
(Katrina picks up bowls and pantomimes washing them in sink.)

Katrina: Would you like me to add wood to the fire for the night? I want to be sure the animals are warm.

The Girl Who Would Be Queen *(cont.)*

Act 1
(cont.)

Old Woman: Yes, thank you. There is wood just outside the front door. *(Katrina goes out the door and goes offstage, returning with a couple of logs. She goes directly to the fireplace and places them there. As she pets the animals, she speaks.)*

Katrina: Is there anything more I can do for you?

Old Woman: No, my dear. You've done enough. You must be tired. I'll show you to your bed. *(Old Woman opens the door facing back of stage, and Katrina enters.)* Sleep well.

Katrina: Good night, and thanks for letting me stay. *(She closes the door.)*

Cow: Is she the one?

Old Woman: Yes, she is. We will reveal our true selves to her in the morning. *(curtain closes)*

Act 2

Setting: beautiful castle, Katrina lying in bed

Narrator 2: When Katrina awoke the next morning, she found herself in a beautiful room. A queen and three princes, all dressed in royal clothes and wearing crowns, stood around her bed.

Katrina: *(sitting up in bed, startled)* Where am I? Who are you? Where are the old woman and her animals?

Queen: Calm down, dear. You are in my castle. These are my sons—Prince Edward, Prince Matthew, and Prince John. Through my magical powers we became an old woman, a cow, a pig, and a sheep.

Prince Edward: Our mother wanted to find a wife for each of us.

Queen: And I have chosen you, Katrina.

Katrina: But . . . but why? I am not a princess.

The Girl Who Would Be Queen *(cont.)*

Act 2
(cont.)

Queen: You have the qualities of a queen. You are polite, humble, and above all, thoughtful. You showed concern for the animals. One who is kind to animals will be kind to her subjects as well.

Prince Matthew: You will stay here for two months. At the end of that time, you will choose one of us to marry.

Prince John: The one you choose will become the king.

Queen: *(nodding)* I could not choose among my sons. You have a good heart, Katrina. You will choose wisely.

Katrina: But what about the two sons I don't choose?

Queen: We'll be at your wedding. Then we will go into the forest, and I will work my magic again to find two more maidens just as we found you.

Katrina: I don't know what to say.

Prince Edward: Just promise to stay the two months and get to know us.

Prince Matthew: Your are sure to fall in love with one of us.

Prince John: Say you'll choose me!

Katrina: Let me go to my parents and tell them what has happened so they won't worry. Then I will come back and after two months, I will choose one of you to marry.

Three Princes: *(throwing their crowns into the air)* Hooray!

Narrator 2: So it came to pass that Katrina became queen and Matthew the king. And the Queen's magic did work twice more to find wonderful wives for Prince Edward and Prince John.

The End

A Celebration of Nursery Rhymes

Teacher's Note: In each of these skits, ALL means the entire class except for those acting out the rhyme. You can present all eight rhymes or choose only the specific ones your class really enjoys.

This Little Piggy

Cast

Piggy 1   _____

Piggy 2   _____   (costumes for all pigs: pages 23–28)

Piggy 3   _____

Piggy 4   _____

Piggy 5   _____

Props: shopping bag with handles, table and chair, plate, fork, "roast beef", cardboard house front with a door cut in it

(Piggy 1 enters from the right and walks across stage carrying a shopping bag. Exits on the left.)

All: This little piggy went to market.

(Piggy 2 waves goodbye from the door of a house and then goes in.)

All: This little piggy stayed home.

(Piggy 3 enters from right and sits at a table and pantomimes eating.)

All: This little piggy had roast beef.

(Piggy 4 enters from the right and goes to Piggy 3 at the table. Piggy 3 shows him the empty plate and shrugs.)

All: But this little piggy had none.

(Piggy 5 enters from the left and rubs his eyes as if crying. He then runs to the door of the house.)

All: And this little piggy cried, "Wee, wee, wee, all the way home."

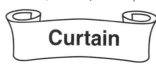

Curtain

A Celebration of Nursery Rhymes *(cont.)*

Mrs. Hen's Chicks
Cast

Woman	_____	(costume: regular clothes)
Mrs. Hen	_____	(costume: pages 17–19)
Yellow Chick	_____	(costumes for all chicks: pages 17–19)
Yellow Chick	_____	
Yellow Chick	_____	
Yellow Chick	_____	
Brown Chick	_____	
Brown Chick	_____	
Brown Chick	_____	
Brown Chick	_____	
Speckled Chick	_____	
Speckled Chick	_____	

Props: none needed

(Woman enters from the left, and Mrs. Hen, followed by her chicks, enters from the right. They meet in center stage.

Woman: Good morning, Mrs. Hen. How many chicks do you have?

Mrs. Hen: Madam, I have ten. Four of them are yellow. *(As the first yellow chick steps forward, it says "one," the second, "two," and so on.)*
Four of them are brown. *(As the first brown chick steps forward, it says, "one," the second, "two," and so on.)*
And two of them are speckled red. *(First speckled chick steps forward and says, "one," and the second steps forward and says, "two.")*

They are the prettiest chicks in town!

Curtain

A Celebration of Nursery Rhymes *(cont.)*

Baa, Baa, Black Sheep

Cast

Black Sheep	_____	(costume: page 38)
Man	_____	(regular clothes)
Master	_____	(regular clothes)
Dame	_____	(regular clothes)
Little Boy	_____	(regular clothes)

Props: three burlap sacks or trash bags stuffed with newspaper

(Black sheep carrying three stuffed burlap sacks enters from left, man from the right. They meet in center stage.)

Man: Baa, baa, Black Sheep, have you any wool?

Sheep: Yes, sir. Yes, sir. Three bags full. One for my master. *(Master enters from the right, takes a bag from the sheep, bows in gratitude, and steps back.)* And one for my dame. *(Dame enters from the right, takes a bag from the sheep, bows in gratitude, and steps back.)* And one for the little boy who lives down the lane. (Little Boy enters from the right, takes a bag from the sheep, bows in gratitude, and steps back.)*

Man: Baa, baa, Black Sheep, have you any wool?

Sheep: Yes, sir. Yes, sir. Three bags full!

Curtain

A Celebration of Nursery Rhymes *(cont.)*

Little Boy Blue

Cast

Little Boy Blue   _____   (costume: blue clothes)

Cows   _____   (costumes: pages 29–31)

                 _____

Sheep   _____   (costumes: page 38)

                 _____

Flowers   _____   (costumes: pages 68–73)

                 _____

Girl   _____   (regular clothes)

Props: three bales of hay, cornstalks.

(When the curtain opens, the little boy dressed in blue is to the front right of the stage, sleeping by some bales of hay. The flowers are standing toward the rear center of the stage with the sheep scattered among them. The cornstalks are standing near the front left of the stage with the cows standing among them.)

All: Little Boy Blue, come blow your horn! The sheep's in the meadow! *(Sheep join arms with the flowers and twirl around.)* The cow's in the corn! *(Cows dance a jig in the corn.)*

Where IS the boy who looks after the sheep? *(Girl comes on stage from the left and creeps slowly toward the haystack.)*

Girl: Why, he's under the haystack, fast asleep!

All: Will you wake him?

Girl: *(shaking her head)* No, not I. For if I do, he'll surely cry!

Curtain

A Celebration of Nursery Rhymes *(cont.)*

Little Bo Peep
Cast

Little Bo Peep   _____   (regular clothes)

Sheep   _____   (costume: page 38)

_____

_____

_____

_____

_____

Props: shepherd's crook, if available

(Little Bo Peep comes onstage holding her hand above her eyes and looking all around for her missing sheep. Behind her back, the sheep come quietly creeping up.)

All: Little Bo Peep has lost her sheep

and can't tell where to find them.

Leave them alone, and they'll come home,

wagging their tails behind them.

(All the sheep stop in their tracks, turn their backs to the audience and shake their tails. When the audience laughs, Little Bo Peep whirls around and acts delighted to see her lost sheep, petting each one in turn.)

Curtain

A Celebration of Nursery Rhymes *(cont.)*

Mary Had a Little Lamb
Cast

Mary _____ (regular clothes)

Little Lamb _____ (costume: page 38)

Classmates _____ (regular clothes)

Teacher _____ (regular clothes)

Props: schoolhouse front with a door that opens

(Mary comes on stage, followed by Little Lamb. She stops and strokes the lamb and then walks across the stage, followed by the Little Lamb.)

All: Mary had a little lamb. Its fleece was white as snow.

And everywhere that Mary went, the lamb was sure to go.

(Mary skips down the lane to school with Little Lamb following. She reaches the school door and goes in. The lamb nudges the door open and follows.)

All: It followed her to school one day, which was against the rule.

(Mary and the classmates come forward, pointing at the lamb and pantomiming laughter. The teacher comes out, looking angry and shaking her finger.)

All: It made the children laugh and play to see a lamb at school.

(Teacher takes Little Lamb by the arm and leads it away from the school. Teacher and children go back inside. The lamb returns and waits at the door.)

All: And so the teacher turned it out. But though the teacher turned it out, still it lingered near and waited patiently about until Mary did appear.

(Mary and her classmates all leave school for the day. The teacher also comes to the door. The classmates act surprised that the lamb is still there.)

Classmates: *(to teacher)* Why does the lamb love Mary so?

All: The eager children cried!

Teacher: Because Mary loves the lamb, you know.

All: The teacher did reply.

Curtain

A Celebration of Nursery Rhymes *(cont.)*

Three Little Kittens

Cast

Kitten 1   _____   (costumes for all: pages 46

Kitten 2   _____   and 47)

Kitten 3   _____

Mother Cat _____

Props: rocking chair, knitting needles, ball of yarn, three pairs of mittens, clothesline and six clothespins, boxes *(or other things to hide mittens under)*, a baked pie, bucket of water

(When curtain opens, there is a clothesline hanging toward the rear of the stage. Mother Cat is sitting in a rocking chair at center stage, pantomiming knitting. The three kittens enter and slowly approach her from the right.)

All: Three little kittens, they lost their mittens, and they began to cry.

Kittens: Oh, Mother dear, we sadly fear that we have lost our mittens.

Mother Cat: What? Lost your mittens? You naughty kittens! Then you shall have no pie.

All: Mee-ow, mee-ow, you shall have no pie!
(The three kittens scamper about the stage, looking behind boxes or props, each looking gleeful and waving mittens high overhead when found.)

All: The three little kittens, they found their mittens, and they began to cry . . .

Kittens: Oh, Mother dear, see here, see here, for we have found our mittens!

Mother Cat: Put on your mittens, you silly kittens, and you shall have some pie.

All: Mee-ow, mee-ow, you shall have some pie!

A Celebration of Nursery Rhymes *(cont.)*

Three Little Kittens (cont.)

(Kittens eagerly put on mittens while Mother Cat gets a pie from under her rocking chair.)

All: The three little kittens put on their mittens and soon ate up the pie. *(The kittens pantomime eating pie by digging in with their hands and then looking with dismay at their mittens, still on their hands.)*

Kittens: Oh, Mother dear, we greatly fear that we have dirtied our mittens.

Mother Cat: *(shaking finger at each one as she speaks)* What? Dirtied your mittens? You naughty kittens!

(Kittens give exaggerated sighs and then look down at the floor. Mother Cat goes offstage and returns with a bucket of water and clothespins.)

All: Then they began to sigh. Mee-ow, mee-ow, then they began to sigh. The three little kittens, they washed their mittens and hung them out to dry.

(Kittens do this and then go to where Mother Cat is sitting in the rocker and take her by the arm.)

Kittens: Oh, Mother dear, come look here, for we have washed our mittens.

Mother Cat: What? Washed your mittens? You're good little kittens. Now I smell a rat close by.

All: Mee-ow, mee-ow, we smell a rat close by! *(Mother Cat and kittens drop to all fours and scoot offstage in pursuit of the rat.)*

Curtain

A Celebration of Nursery Rhymes *(cont.)*

Little Robin Redbreast

Cast

Robin   _____   (costume: pages 39–41)

Pussy Cat   _____   (costume: pages 46–47)

Props: stepladder, tree, small trampoline, half wall of sturdy cardboard boxes or constructed of wood and painted to look like cobblestones

Setting: Robin is standing on a stepladder *(which is hidden behind a tree).* There is a trampoline below and a half wall nearby.

All: Little Robin Redbreast sat upon a tree. Up went Pussy Cat, and down went he. *(Pussy Cat goes up ladder, and Robin jumps to trampoline.)*

Down came Pussy, and away Robin ran. *(Pussy Cat jumps down onto trampoline and chases Robin, who runs around.)*

Said Little Robin Redbreast . . .

Robin: *(shouts over shoulder to Pussy Cat in a mocking tone)* Catch me if you can!

All: Little Robin Redbreast jumped upon a wall. Pussy Cat jumped after him and almost had a fall. *(Robin jumps up onto the wall, followed by Pussy Cat, who almost falls off.)*

Little Robin Redbreast chirped . . .

Robin: Chirp, chirp, chirp!

All: And what did Pussy say? Pussy Cat said . . .

Pussy Cat: Mee-ow, mee-ow!

All: And Robin flew away! *(Robin flies offstage.)*

Curtain

Aesop's Fables

Teacher's Note: You may choose to present all 10 fables or select only a few that your class most enjoys. Aesop and his friend remain the same throughout the play.

The Fox and the Grapes

Cast

Aesop   _____   *(costume: toga made from white or buff-colored sheet)*

Aesop's Friend   _____   *(costume: same as Aesop wears)*

Fox   _____   *(costume: pages 50–52)*

Props: tree, bunch of grapes

Setting: tree with a bunch of grapes hanging from it, just out of reach of the jumping fox

Fox: *(He enters from the right and walks toward the tree.)* It's just about lunchtime, and boy, am I hungry! I'd better find some food fast! *(He spies grapes.)*

Well! What have we here? It looks like a delicious bunch of grapes. They would make a perfect lunch for me!

(Fox then jumps four times, trying to grab the grapes unsuccessfully. He then shakes his head and looks out at the audience.)

I bet those grapes are sour anyway! *(Fox exits left. Aesop and his friend come onstage.)*

Aesop: It is easy to scorn something that you want but cannot have!

Aesop's Friend: When you want something you can't have, you may pretend not to want it.

Curtain

Aesop's Fables (cont.)

The Crow and the Fox

Cast

Crow _____ (costume: pages 39–41)

Fox _____ (costume: pages 50–52)

Props: tree, stepladder, large piece of cheese

Setting: tree with a ladder hidden behind it, crow standing on the ladder with a large piece of cheese in its mouth

(Fox enters from the right and walks toward the tree.)

Fox: Hello there, Crow! My, what a fine looking bird you are with your bright eyes and shiny feathers! If only you could speak, you would be the greatest of all the birds!

Crow: *(opens mouth to speak and drops cheese from beak)* Caw! Caw!
(Fox snatches up cheese from the ground.)

Fox: So, you DO have a voice! Too bad you have so little brain! *(Fox exits left, chased by Crow.)*
(Aesop and his friend come onstage.)

Aesop: Don't let flattery go to your head!

Aesop's Friend: Some people will say charming things to you just to get something from you.

Curtain

Aesop's Fables *(cont.)*

The Hen and the Fox
Cast

Hen   _____   (costume: pages 17–19)

Fox   _____   (costume: pages 50–52)

Props: stepladder hidden behind "barn rafters"

Setting: hen roosting on rafters of barn

(Fox enters from the right and goes to the hen, looking up at her.)

Fox: Dear Hen, you don't look as if you feel well, and I fear you may faint. I am worried that you may fall from so high a perch. Please come down right now, and I will take care of you.

Hen: Yes, Fox, I do feel sick today. I feel so sick, in fact, that I'm afraid I might die if I come down!

(Fox, shaking his head, exits right. Hen flaps her wings and exits left.)

(Aesop and his friend come onstage.)

Aesop: Do not be fooled by false concern!

Aesop's Friend: Some people may act like they care about you when they really don't.

Curtain

Aesop's Fables *(cont.)*

The Bundle of Sticks
Cast

Father _____ *(costumes for all: regular clothes)*

Eldest Son _____

Middle Son _____

Youngest Son _____

Props: table, four chairs, bundle of sticks tied with string

Setting: father and three sons seated at a table in center stage

Youngest Son: But, Father, he started it! *(points to Middle Son)*

Middle Son: I did not! Father, he's such a whiner! All he ever does is complain and blame somebody else for his foolishness!

Eldest Son: You're being too harsh! After all, he is only a boy.

Middle Son: You always side with him!

Youngest Son: No, he doesn't. He usually sides with you!

Eldest Son: I do not take sides!

Father: QUIET! My sons, the time is coming when I will no longer be with you. You will have to rely on each other. Yet the way the three of you fight, I cannot imagine you working together. So do this for me. Gather together a bundle of sticks, tie it with string, and bring it here.
(The three sons go offstage, and all immediately return with the eldest carrying a bundle of sticks.)

Eldest Son: Here are the sticks you asked for, Father. What do you want done with them?

Father: Take the bundle just as it is and break it in two. Whichever one of you can do that will inherit everything I own.

Aesop's Fables (cont.)

The Bundle of Sticks (cont.)

(Eldest Son, Middle Son, and Youngest Son each take a turn trying to break the bundle. As each one fails, he shakes his head and then hands it to the next son.)

Youngest Son: Father, you have given us an impossible task!

Father: You are right. *(He reaches for the bundle. Youngest son gives it to him. Father undoes the string around the bundle and removes three sticks. He hands one to each son.)* Now try.
(All three sons easily snap their sticks across their knees.)

Father: It's the same with you, my sons. Together you will be strong. But if you argue and separate, your enemies may ruin you. *(The sons look at one another and nod their heads in agreement. Then they link arms with each other and the father and exit right.*
(Aesop and his friend come on stage.)

Aesop: There is strength in unity!

Aesop's Friend: If we stick together, we can do much more than we can do alone.

Curtain

Aesop's Fables *(cont.)*

The Selfish Bees
Cast

Mother Nature _____   (costume: long white robe or sheet)

Bee 1   _____   (costumes for honeybees: pages 64 and 65)

Bee 2   _____

Bee 3   _____

Bee 4   _____

Bee 5   _____

Props: none needed

Setting: five bees huddle together at right edge of stage

Bee 1: I'm sick and tired of bears and skunks and humans always stealing our honey!

Bee 2: I know what you mean. After all, we're the ones who work so hard to make it.

Bee 3: If only we could chase those pests away.

Bee 4: We need some way to defend our honey!

Bee 5: Let's go ask Mother Nature. She will know what to do!
(Bees cross stage, buzzing loudly. As they near the left edge, Mother Nature enters from the left. They all stop and bow at her entrance and then rise.)

Bee 1: Mother Nature, we were just coming to see you.

Mother Nature: I heard you coming. What do you want?

Bee 2: We need a way to keep the other animals and people away from our honey.

Aesop's Fables *(cont.)*

The Selfish Bees *(cont.)*

Bee 3: We work so hard to make it, and then they come and destroy our hive and steal our honey.

Bee 4: We would like you to give us the power to sting any creature that even comes near our hive.

Mother Nature: But what if the creature doesn't want to take your honey?

Bee 5: We'll sting them anyway! We want all others to fear us! We want them to run when they hear our buzzing!

Mother Nature: Very well, your request is granted. You may sting any creature that you'd like. BUT when you use your sting, it will cost you your own life.
(Bees, looking very unhappy, buzz across the stage and exit right; Mother Nature turns and exits left.)

(Aesop and his friend come on stage.)

Aesop: Selfishness brings its own punishment!

Aesop's Friend: When you act selfishly, you will eventually suffer.

Curtain

Aesop's Fables *(cont.)*

The Too Fat Fox

Cast

First Fox   _____   *(costume for foxes: pages 50–52)*

Second Fox   _____

Props: card table covered with a dark cloth

Setting: cave with an opening *(represented by the cloth-covered table)*

(First Fox enters from the right, sniffing around.)

First Fox: I'm so hungry I could eat a horse! I think I smell meat around here somewhere. *(spies cave)* Aha! *(Dashes over and disappears under the table with the cloth closing around him. Sounds of lip-smacking and eating and yum-yumming come from within the "cave.")*

First Fox: *(sticking head out of curtain)* Aaah . . . I feel much better! *(Tries to get out, but seems to be stuck.)* What's going on here? I can't get out! Oh, no! My stomach has gotten so big that I'm stuck in here! What'll I do?

(Second Fox enters from the left and approaches the cave.)

First Fox: Please, help me!

Second Fox: What's the matter?

First Fox: I came in here and ate a feast. Now I am stuck and cannot escape. Please grab my leg and pull me out. *(Second Fox tries to pull out First Fox but cannot budge him. Second Fox starts to walk away.)*

First Fox: Wait! Stop! You can't leave me stuck in here!

Second Fox: *(stops walking and shrugs shoulders)* What else can be done? You'll just have to stay there until your stomach shrinks. Then you'll be able to get out as easily as you got in. *(Second Fox exits, and First Fox groans, then pulls back inside the cave and is no longer visible.)*

(Aesop and his friend come onstage.)

Aesop: Time solves many problems!

Aesop's Friend: Lots of problems just take care of themselves if you give them enough time.

Curtain

Aesop's Fables *(cont.)*

The Rejected Bird
Cast

Proud Mardi Gras Bird   _____   (costumes: pages 42–43)

Mardi Gras Bird 1   _____

Mardi Gras Bird 2   _____

Mardi Gras Bird 3   _____

Crow 1   _____   (costumes: pages 39–41)

Crow 2   _____

Crow 3   _____

Props: two separate trees or bunches of branches

Setting: Four Mardi Gras birds are huddled in front of a tree toward the front of the stage. There is another tree on the other side of the stage toward the back.

Proud Mardi Gras Bird: I am the largest, most beautiful bird of our whole flock. None of you can compare to me. *(struts around in front of other birds)*

Mardi Gras Bird 1: I like my size just fine.

Mardi Gras Bird 2: I think I'm a pretty bird.

Mardi Gras Bird 3: If you think you're so much better than the rest of us, why don't you leave us alone and go join another flock?

Proud MG Bird: Well, that's the first good idea you've ever had! I will go join the crows. I'm sure they will appreciate my size and beauty. *(He flies over to the other tree. Crows "fly" onstage and gather around that tree.)*

Crow 1: What are YOU doing here?

Aesop's Fables *(cont.)*

The Rejected Bird (cont.)

Proud MG Bird: I want to join your flock. I'm sure you'll be delighted to have such a large, gorgeous bird as myself in your group. *(struts around in front of the crows)*

Crow 2: Are you kidding? You are the weirdest looking thing I've ever seen!

Crow 3: You're way too big and flashy for us crows. We like plain, simple black feathers.

Crow 1: You look like a leftover from a carnival.

Crow 2: Talk about gaudy!

Crow 3: Why don't you leave us alone and go back to your own kind?

Proud MG Bird: Well, that's the first good thing you've said to me! I will go rejoin my friends. They are far better to me than you are. *(flies over to the other tree)*

MG Bird 1: What are you doing back?

MG Bird 2: Didn't the crows appreciate your size and beauty?

MG Bird 3: I thought you said you were too good for us.

Proud MG Bird: I am sorry that I was mean to you. I want to rejoin the flock.

All MG Birds: Forget it! Get lost! *(Proud MG Bird flaps slowly off stage to left. The three MG Birds flap off to the right.)*

(Aesop and Friend come on stage.)

Aesop: You cannot expect those you have insulted to welcome you!

Aesop's Friend: Very true. You can't be rude to people and then expect them to be your friends.

Curtain

134

Aesop's Fables *(cont.)*

The Goat and the Fox

Cast

Goat _____ (costume: pages 33–37)

Fox _____ (costume: pages 50–52)

Props: large barrel painted to look like a cobblestone well

Setting: Fox is in a well *(barrel).*

Fox: *(to the audience)* This is a fine mess I've gotten into! I fell into this well when I leaned over too far to get a drink. I don't know how I'll get out!

(Goat enters from the right and comes up to the well.)

Fox: *(behind hand to audience)* Let's see if I can trick this goat into getting me out. *(Fox turns to Goat.)*

Fox: Hello, Goat!

Goat: What are you doing?

Fox: I'm drinking the best water I ever tasted! Say, there's plenty for us both. Won't you join me?

(Goat jumps into barrel. Fox scrambles up onto Goat's back and climbs out of the barrel.)

Goat: Hey, what about me? How am I supposed to get out?

Fox: You should have thought of that before you jumped in. *(Fox exits to the left. Goat is left in the "well.")*

(Aesop and Friend come onstage.)

Aesop: Always look before you leap!

Aesop's Friend: Yes, before you do something, always think about what might happen.

Curtain

Aesop's Fables (cont.)

The Pig and the Cat

Cast

Pig _____ (costume: pages 23-28)

Cat _____ (costume: pages 46 and 47)

Props: stuffed kitten and stuffed piglet

(Pig enters from the right, carrying a stuffed piglet. Cat enters from the left, carrying a stuffed kitten. They meet in the center of the stage.)

Pig: Hello there, friend Cat! Come see my fine new baby. Isn't he the most beautiful thing you've ever seen? *(Pig holds out stuffed animal for Cat and audience to get a better look.)*

Cat: Your piglet cannot compare to my lovely kitten. She is the most beautiful thing I've ever seen. *(Cat holds up stuffed animal for pig and audience to get a better look.)*

Pig: Your kitten may be pretty, but she does not have my piglet's fine pink skin.

Cat: Well, your piglet does not have my kitten's soft fur!

Pig: Your kitten has a squashed little nose!

Cat: Far better than that awful long snout on your piglet!

Pig: At least my baby could see from the moment he was born. Yours is still as blind as a bat!

Cat: *(turns and walks away in a huff but shouts back over her shoulder . . .)* I shall never speak to you again, Pig. You are no friend of mine! *(Cat exits left. Pig exits right.)*

(Aesop and Friend come on stage.)

Aesop: Needless comparisons can lead to ruined relationships!

Aesop's Friend: True! Do not brag, for it can hurt others' feelings and you might lose friends.

Curtain

Aesop's Fables *(cont.)*

The Wise Bear

Cast

Friend 1   _____ (costumes: regular clothes)

Friend 2   _____

Bear   _____ (costume: pages 61–62)

Props: stepladder hidden behind a tree

Setting: a forest path with a tree (ladder behind)

(Two friends enter from right, walking slowly toward the tree.)

Friend 1: It's a lovely day for a walk with my best friend. *(links arms with Friend 2)*

Friend 2: Yes, and I feel lucky to have such a good friend to share it with! *(Bear enters from left and heads toward friends.)*

Friend 1: Run for your life! *(He drops friend's arm and runs to tree, racing up ladder. Friend 2 freezes.)*

Friend 2: Help! Help!

(Friend 2 starts to run to the tree, but Bear blocks his or her path. Friend 2 falls to the ground and plays dead. Bear drops to all fours and sniffs all around Friend 2, then whispers something into the ear of Friend 2, and finally lumbers offstage on the right. Friend 2 sits up and wipes brow in relief. Friend 1 comes down from the tree and comes over to Friend 2.)

Friend 1: What did that bear whisper in your ear?

Friend 2: He said that I should choose friends who stick by me when there is danger. *(Friend 1 hangs head and exits to the right. Friend 2 gets up, dusts self off, and exits left.)*

(Aesop and Friend come on stage.)

Aesop: A true friend will not desert you, even in the face of danger.

Aesop's Friend: Real friends will stick with you, no matter what.

Curtain

Bee-ing a Bee

(Based on information from The Life and Times of the Honeybee *by Charles Micucci, Houghton Mifflin, 1995)*

Teacher's Note: This can be a whole-class play with children taking multiple roles or a two-class play. It also works well as a multi-age play with the older children doing the narration and the younger ones doing the acting. If there are too many parts, have the same worker bees for different months. You can omit the flower actors and make large flowers instead.

Since the narration parts are long, the narrators should read from cards. Make certain they read slowly since reading too fast is a common mistake of young narrators.

The narrator reads the information for each month while the bee actors pantomime the activities described.

Cast

Narrator 1   _____ (costumes: regular clothes)

Narrator 2   _____

Narrator 3   _____

First Queen Bee   _____ (costumes: pages 64 and 65; add crown, page 74)

New Queen Bee   _____ (costumes: pages 64 and 65; add crown, page 74)

Flower 1   _____ (costumes for all: pages 68–73; color like cherry blossoms)

Flower 1   _____

Flower 1   _____

Flower 2   _____ (costumes for all: pages 68–73; color like white clovers)

Flower 2   _____

Flower 2   _____

Bee-ing a Bee *(cont.)*

Cast *(cont.)*

January Bees   _____   (costumes: pages 64 and 65)

_____

_____

February Bees   _____   (must be a boy, needs a bow tie)

_____   (must be a boy, needs a bow tie)

_____   (must be a boy, needs a bow tie)

March Bee   _____   (costumes: pages 64 and 65)

_____

_____

April Bees   _____   (costumes: pages 64 and 65)

_____

_____

May Bees   _____   (costumes: pages 64 and 65)

_____

_____

June Bees   _____   (must be a girl with a pink ribbon)

_____   (must be a boy with a blue ribbon)

_____

_____

_____

Bee-ing a Bee *(cont.)*

Cast *(cont.)*

July Bees   _____ (costumes: pages 64 and 65)

_____

_____

August Bees   _____ (costumes: pages 64 and 65)

_____

_____

September Bees   _____ (costumes: pages 64 and 65)

_____

_____

October Bees   _____ (costumes: pages 64 and 65)

_____

_____

November Bees   _____ (costumes: pages 64 and 65)

_____

_____

December Bees   _____ (costumes: pages 64 and 65)

_____

_____

Bee-ing a Bee *(cont.)*

Props: three chairs for narrators; large backdrop of yellow cloth or butcher paper with hexagonal patterns drawn in black; 72 empty boxes—e.g., shoeboxes or copier paper cartons *(stacked four high by 18 wide)* painted yellow both interior and exterior; 72 inflated, long (not round), yellow balloons with black stripes drawn on them with permanent marker; three bow ties; one blue bow and one pink bow for children's heads; three caulking guns

Setting: lots of yellow boxes stacked about two or three high and close together in front of the yellow backdrop with the hexagon outlines to resemble a hive

(Three narrators come on stage and sit off to one side. As each one reads, he or she stands and then sits down when done.)

Narrator 1: You've heard the saying "busy as a bee." Well, today we're going to show you what that means. You'll find out what it's like "bee-ing a bee."

(First Queen Bee and January Bees come onstage and go to the center. They huddle around the Queen, moving their wings rapidly. They all make motions as if they are eating.)

Narrator 2: Honeybees live on every continent except Antarctica. They are busy all year round. In January, the bees eat the honey they have stored in their hive. During the winter the average bee colony eats at least 50 pounds of honey.

(January Bees exit and February Bees wearing bow ties enter. First Queen Bee takes a turn dancing with each of the drones.)

Narrator 3: In February, the queen bee mates with newborn male bees, called drones. Then she starts laying eggs. During her lifetime, she may lay as many as one million eggs.

(February Bees exit, and First Queen Bee begins putting inflated yellow balloons with black stripes drawn on them into boxes near the back of the stage. While she's doing this, March Bees enter, tap First Queen Bee on the shoulder to get her attention, and wave goodbye. Then they exit.)

Bee-ing a Bee *(cont.)*

Narrator 1: During March, if the temperature reaches 54° F (12° C), female bees called workers leave the hive to search for flowers. But in northern areas, they will probably only find crocuses and snowdrops, neither of which has a good supply of pollen or nectar.

(Flower 1s enter from left and stand very still. April Bees enter from the right and go immediately to the flowers. They rub against them, buzzing loudly. They buzz back to First Queen Bee at the comb and then buzz off the stage.)

Narrator 2: Field worker bees spend many hours each April day gathering nectar and pollen from early-blooming spring flowers, especially cherry blossoms. Bees then change the nectar into honey, which they eat for energy. They store the pollen to eat for protein.

(New Queen Bee comes out from behind the boxes First Queen Bee has been filling with balloons. The May Bees come onstage and escort First Queen Bee off, all buzzing loudly. Flower 1s exit on opposite side.)

Narrator 3: Each May a new queen is born. The old queen and about half of the worker bees leave the hive and fly in a swarm to build a new hive and start a new colony. Queens generally live about four years. All other bees live between six and 16 weeks.

(Flower 2s come onstage and stand very still. The February Bees come back onstage and lounge about on the floor. Two June Bees come onstage, fly to Flower 1s and rub against them and then fly back to the comb. Two June Bees wait at the comb to receive honey and pollen from field bees and then turn and feed it to two "baby" June bees seated in front of the boxes. The boy baby wears a blue bow around his neck; the girl baby wears a pink bow around her neck. The same two June Bees then tend to the February bees.)

Narrator 1: June is the month when field worker bees get nectar and pollen from white clover, their favorite flower. The hive worker bees are responsible for feeding the baby bees a mixture of honey and pollen called *beebread*. The lazy drones hang around in the hive and won't even feed themselves. They wait for the worker bees to feed them.

Bee-ing a Bee *(cont.)*

(February Bees exit. June Bees stay onstage and follow New Queen Bee, who is putting yellow inflated balloons with black stripes drawn on them into the boxes at the rear of the stage. Flower 1s enter from the left and stand very still next to Flower 2s. July Bees enter from the right. They immediately go to the flowers, rubbing against them and buzzing loudly.)

Narrator 2: July is one of the most productive months for bees. They make more honey in July, August, and September than in all the rest of the year. This is also the time when the queen lays the most eggs—as many as 1,500 per day. This is very tiring for the queen, so 12 worker bees guard, clean, and feed her.

(June and July Bees exit. August Bees come on stage and use caulking guns to pretend to seal the cells on the honeycomb backdrop.)

Narrator 3: During August, the worker bees use bee glue to mend cracks around the brood cells where bee larvae are developing. These same bees store honey around the cells, too. Worker bees are the hardest working of all the bees. They make the honeycomb out of beeswax, gather and store all the honey and pollen, take care of the baby bees, and guard the hive.

(August Bees exit. September Bees come onstage and RUSH back and forth between the flowers and hive, buzzing loudly. February Bees come onstage, tap New Queen on the shoulder to get her attention, then wave goodbye sadly, and with heads hanging, exit.)

Narrator 1: In September, the field worker bees spend every daylight moment visiting as many flowers as possible before the autumn chill. A field worker bee may stop at 600 flowers in one day. Toward the end of September, the drones leave the hive and die because they are no longer needed. Keeping them alive would take too much honey, and new drones will be born for the next mating season.

(September Bees exit. October Bees come onstage. Two go to the flowers, and two use the caulking guns on the honeycomb backdrop.)

Bee-ing a Bee *(cont.)*

Narrator 2: When October comes, the field workers busily collect nectar from autumn flowers such as goldenrod, asters, and mums. All through the summer, the field worker bees have gathered nectar and pollen for use as food during the long winter season. Now they also bring back water and plant sap for use in sealing the hive against bad weather.

(Flower 1s and Flower 2s and October Bees exit. November Bees come onstage. New Queen Bee stops putting balloons into boxes and collapses into the arms of November Bees. They lay her gently on the floor and kneel around her.)

Narrator 3: Sometime in November, the queen stops laying eggs. These last eggs will produce the drones for her next mating season in late winter.

(December Bees come onstage and join November Bees around New Queen Bee. They pull her up into a standing position and then gather around her very closely and rapidly move their wings.)

Narrator 1: The weather grows colder every day in December. The worker bees gather closely around their queen and rapidly move their wings to keep her warm.

(All Bees, Flowers, and First Queen Bee come onstage. Everyone joins hands.)

Narrator 2: Honeybees are very useful insects. For more than 10,000 years people have used their beeswax for candles and their honey for food.

Narrator 3: Today, the most important role of honeybees is pollinating the plants that give us fruits and vegetables. Without them, America's crops would be cut by one-third. That means that instead of 10 ears of corn, there would only be seven. We're very glad we have honeybees!

(All Bees, Queens, and Flowers take a bow together.)

Curtain